SELECTIONS
FROM
ITALIAN
POETRY

Illustrations by ANN GRIFALCONI

851
08
De

SELECTIONS
FROM
ITALIAN POETRY

A Bilingual Selection

By A. MICHAEL DE LUCA

and WILLIAM GIULIANO

Foreword by Thomas G. Bergin

HARVEY HOUSE, INC.
Publishers
Irvington-on-Hudson, N.Y.

67-03376

To Rose and Esther

Library of Congress Catalog Card Number: AC 66-10394
Manufactured in the United States of America

HARVEY HOUSE, INC. • Publishers
Irvington-on-Hudson • New York

Foreword

The lyric voice of Italy, according to Leopardi, has its birth in tears. As the reader of *Selections from Italian Poetry* glances through the first few selections, he may readily conclude that its origins are in pantheistic rapture, extreme irascibility, or idealistic love. Leopardi was thinking poetically, having in mind the melancholy of Petrarch, who stands at the fountainhead of a great current of inspiration (not only for Italy) ; historically he is on less firm ground. The fact is that *l'italo canto,* or in plain English, Italian poetry, contains from the beginning all the themes that echo the hopes, aspirations, and questionings of the human heart. Do Italian poets necessarily voice these emotions better than poets of other great literatures? Of course not, but Italian poets express themselves in a music uniquely their own, and not infrequently with a taste and delicacy that has made them, at recurrent intervals in our history, spokesmen for all of us and teachers of the "wordsmiths" of other nations. At other moments, Italian singers have been quite willing to pick up suggestions from abroad, but in doing so, they have never failed to give the importations their own characteristic stamp. Over the seven and a half centuries that have passed since St. Francis of Assisi unforgettably accepted his universe with joy and charity, there have been poets in Italy, and good ones, as all the world knows, many more good ones than the world remembers. If there have been the great voices we have already alluded to, there also have been hosts of others who have not had the recognition they deserve.

This anthology that has been prepared by Professors De Luca and Giuliano will be welcome to all who know something of the long tradition of Italian verse. It will also be useful and appealing to those who are as yet unfamiliar with the vitality, the elegance and the range of the poetry of Italy. The fifty-seven poems chosen are representative of various literary periods. These are arranged in chronological order, thus making them pedagogically convenient and useful for the historical approach.

Both the items chosen and the proportions assigned to various literary periods are interesting, as indicative of the editors' purpose. The fifty-seven selections are taken from the works of only twenty-nine poets, thirteen of whom have more than one item. Thus it has been possible, in a relatively small compass, to concentrate on the few and to seek for quality rather than quantity. Happily, the selections contain a great variety of themes: there are love poems, religious poems, patriotic poems, and poems reflecting public attitudes, as well as poems of deeply personal meaning. In tone they range from the devotional to the burlesque; in style from simplicity to challenging subtlety. If the collection is small and deliberately designed to be so in order to present a manageable, or as one might say, an intimate book, there is certainly no lack of variety in its contents.

The translations have been chosen, or in a number of cases especially made, to make the reader feel, through the English, something of the delight afforded by the original Italian.

Concise informational material has been prepared, and some editorial aids have been offered to the reader. But I am happy to say that such matters, useful though they be, have been kept to a minimum. The intention of the editors has been simply to enlarge the circle, already great, but not so great as it should be, of lovers of Italian verse. There are many treasures beyond those contained in these few pages. It is, I am sure, the hope of the editors that their readers will be eager to seek further. But as an antipasto—if I may be forgiven the figure—this selection, tastefully and judiciously prepared, should serve its purpose well.

THOMAS G. BERGIN

Yale University
New Haven, Connecticut
October, 1966

Preface

The most casual survey of Italy's literary history will reveal a preponderance of poetry over prose. Its earliest literary movements—the Sicilian School and that of *Il Dolce stil nuovo* (Sweet New Style) in the twelfth, thirteenth, and early fourteenth centuries—were exclusively devoted to poetry. Between 1265 and 1375, Italy achieved a preeminence in poetry as a consequence of the work of three literary giants who lived in that period, Dante, Petrarch and Boccaccio. This preeminence was destined to transcend the Italian borders and to exert a marked influence on the poetry of the West.

With his *Divine Comedy*, Dante has endured for seven centuries as the symbol and mainspring of Italy's lyrical genius, and he was singled out by T. S. Eliot as "the most universal of poets in the modern languages." With rare exception, Italy's poets—from the origins to Salvatore Quasimodo,

Nobel Prize winner for literature in 1959—have appealed to all mankind and, particularly, to the English-speaking community.

This bilingual *Selections from Italian Poetry* is another expression of affinity in a grand tradition, which began with Geoffrey Chaucer and continues vigorously among American and British men of letters of our times.

We, the editors, have audaciously attempted to present a swift panorama of Italian poetry, a task which, in view of the massive accumulation across time, is akin to emptying the sea into a sand pail. Our efforts have been guided by the general criterion of offering to poetry lovers and to students representative poems from every period of Italian literature which are cherished in Italy and elsewhere. Since ours is a sampling, it implies arbitrary choice, and an omission, unfortunately, of many worthy poets whose inclusion undoubtedly would have been assured by other compilers.

We have included a number of poetic translations by distinguished poets, such as Henry W. Longfellow, Lord Byron, Dante Gabriel Rossetti, Leigh Hunt, and others, so that the reader who is not acquainted with Italian will derive a lyrical appreciation of the originals. However, since the restrictions of meter and rhyme oblige poetic translators to take certain liberties with the originals, we have provided many line-by-line translations of our own, which are closer to the originals. Closer but never perfect, for it is a truism that no translator can ever render precisely the beauty and emotional qualities of an original, or, as the Italians express it: *Traduttore—traditore* ("Translator—traitor").

The brief sketches on the authors and their works are not intended for the literary scholar, but for new readers of Italian poetry, or for others who may wish to renew their acquaintance with it. It is hoped that these sketches, along with the poems themselves, will serve as an incentive to the reader to broaden not only his knowledge of Italian poetry, but also as a preview of the rich rewards of Italian literature in general. We are hopeful, also, that the reader who does not already know Italian will be stimulated to study this most musical of languages.

Great enjoyment may be derived from reciting the poems aloud, which may be done with relative ease, since Italian is not difficult to pronounce. To facilitate pronunciation for non-Italian speakers, a brief summary of the rules of pronunciation have been provided.

A.M.D.
W.G.

A Simple Guide to Italian Pronunciation

1. CONSONANTS PRONOUNCED APPROXIMATELY AS IN ENGLISH
   These are b, d, f, l, m, n, p, t, and v. The pronunciation of the other consonants will be explained further ahead.

2. THE VOWELS
   Italian vowels are clean-cut, never slurred and pronounced without the off-glide which is common in English.

a   like *a* in *father*: *lana, dama*

e   sometimes like *a* in *day*: *fede, mela;* sometimes like *e* in *met*: *è, Etna.* This distinction is not always kept, but final *e* is almost invariably like the first type.

i   like *i* in *machine*: *bambini, vini*

o   sometimes like *o* in *rope*: *nome, lavoro;* sometimes like *u* in *cut*: *moda, volta.* This distinction is not always kept, but final *o* is almost invariably like the first type.

u   like *oo* in *moon*: *luna, ultimo*

3. OTHER CONSONANTS AND CONSONANT COMBINATIONS

c   before *a, o,* and *u,* like English k: *cane, coda, cupola*

c   before *e* and *i,* soft like *ch* in church: *cena, cinema*
    In the combinations *cia, cio, ciu* the *i* is silent: *cominciare, ciuco*

c   before *he* and *hi,* like English k: *perchè, chilo*

g   before *a, o,* and *u,* hard as in English: *lago, gusto* g   before *e* and *i*, soft as in English: *angelo, Gina*

     In the combinations *gia, gio,* and *giu,* the *i* is silent: *giovane, giusto*

g   before *he* and *hi*, hard like English *go: fughe, laghi*

gl   before *i*, approximately like English *lli* in *million*. It produces the same sound before *ia, ie, io* and *iu*, the *i* being silent: *figli, figlia, figliuolo, glielo*

gn like *ni* in *union: bagno, vergogna*

h   is always silent

qu as in English: *questo, quando*

r   unlike English. It is trilled and produced by a single flap of the tongue. It approximates the sound most Americans make in pronouncing the word *muddy: cura, tirare*

s   like *s* in *sin* when initial, double, and before *c, f, p,* and *t: solo, rosso, scala, spada*

s   like *s* in *rose* when single between two vowels (except *casa* and *cosa*) and before *b, d, g, l, m, n, r,* and *v; rosa, snello*

sc like English *sh* before *e* and *i: pesce, conosci;* before *ia, ie, io, iu* the *i* is silent: *conosciamo, scienza*

sc before *he* and *hi*, like English *sk: pesche, dischi*

4. Double Consonants

In Italian double consonants are pronounced more vigorously than single consonants. The sound of the double consonant is held longer than for the single consonant: *ballo, sonno, terra, letto, buffo*

5. Stress, Accent and Apostrophe

Italian words are usually stressed on the next-to-the-last syllable: *dolce, cantare, signorina*

Some words are stressed on the last syllable and have the grave accent mark (`) over the final vowel: *perchè, virtù, verità*

Some words are stressed on the third-from-the-last and the fourth-from-the-last syllable: *parlano, telefonano.*

Written accents are used on certain monosyllabic words to distinguish them from others of similar spelling and different meanings: *nè*-nor, from *ne*-some; *sè*-himself, from *se*-if; *è*-he or she is, from *e*-and.

An apostrophe is employed in Italian to denote the ommission of a vowel. Usually apostrophized words are joined with words following them in a single and blended pronunciation: *l'albero, c'è, D'Annunzio.*

Acknowledgments

The editors and publishers are grateful for the cooperation of those individuals and publishers who granted permission to use their copyrighted material. Every effort has been made to trace and to acknowledge properly all copyright owners. If any acknowledgment has been inadvertently omitted, the publishers will be pleased to make necessary corrections in the next printing.

Excerpts from Canto III and Canto V of the *Divine Comedy* of Dante Alighieri, translated from the Italian by Jefferson B. Fletcher; New York, Columbia University Press, 1931. Reprinted by permission of the publisher.

"Clear, Fresh, and Dulcet Streams," translated from the Italian of Francesco Petrarca by Leigh Hunt; in L. R. Lind, *Lyric Poetry of the Italian Renaissance*, New Haven, Yale University Press, 1954.

"Morning," from *The Day, A Poem by Giuseppe Parini*, translated from the Italian by Herbert Morris Bower; London, Routledge and Kegan Paul, Ltd., 1927. Reprinted by permission of the publisher.

"The Infinite" and "Saturday in the Village," translated from the Italian by Jean-Pierre Barricelli, in *The Poetry of Giacomo Leopardi*; New York, Las Americas Publishing Co., 1963. Reprinted by permission of the publisher.

"Crossing the Tuscan Maremma" and "A Snow-Storm," translated from the Italian by G. L. Bickersteth; in *Giosuè Carducci, A Selection of His Poems*; London, Longmans Green and Co., 1913. Reprinted by permission of the publisher.

"Il gelsomino notturno," from *Canti di Castelvecchio* by Giovanni Pascoli. © copyright 1953 by Arnoldo Mondadori Editore, Milan. Reprinted by permission of the publisher.

"Falce di luna" and "La pioggia nel pineto" by Gabriele D'Annunzio; in Francesco Flora, *Il fiore della lirica di D'Annunzio*. © copyright 1958 by Arnoldo Mondadori Editore, Milan. Reprinted and translated by permission of the publisher.

"Alle soglie," from *Poesie e prose* by Guido Gozzano; Milan, Garzanti Editore, 1960. Reprinted by permission of the copyright owner, Renato Gozzano, Turin.

"La fontana malata" by Aldo Palazzeschi, in *Opere giovanili*. © copyright 1959 by Arnoldo Mondadori Editore, Milan. Reprinted by permission of the publisher.

"The Ailing Fountain," translated from the Italian by Carlo L. Golino, reprinted with the permission of the copyright owners, the Regents of the University of California, from Carlo L. Golino, *Contemporary Italian Poetry*, University of California Press, 1962.

Grateful acknowledgment is made to the Research Committee of C. W. Post College of Long Island University for its financial assistance in the physical preparation of the manuscript.

Contents

Canticle of the Lord's Creations

Most high, almighty and benign Lord,
Thine is the praise, the glory, the honor
And every blessing.
On Thee, only, O Heavenly Lord, can they be bestowed
For no man is worthy even to utter Thy name.

Praised be Thou, my Lord, and all Thy creations
And especially lord brother sun
Who rises daily and brings us Thy light.
He is handsome and shines with brilliant radiance
And because of Thee, O Heavenly Lord, he bears meaning.

Praised by Thou, my Lord, for sister moon and the stars;
In the heavens hast Thou formed them, bright, precious and beautiful.

Praised be Thou, my Lord, for brother wind
And for the air, clouds, clear skies and every weather
By which Thou givest sustenance to all Thy creatures.

Praised be Thou, my Lord, for sister water
Who is very useful, humble, precious and pure . . .

Praised be Thou, my Lord, for our sister corporeal death
From whom no living man can escape;
Woe to those who will die in mortal sin,
Blessed be those whom death will encounter in Thy holy grace
For thus second death to them will bring no harm.

Praise and bless my Lord, and thank him
And serve him with all humility.

Translated by W. G.

San Francesco d'Assisi (c. 1182-1226), founder of the Franciscan order, expresses his well-known love of nature in this simple but beautiful poem. Strong traces of the saint's native Umbrian dialect are present in the Italian of this poem. The complete composition contains thirty-four lines.

Altissumu, omnipotente, bon Signore
Tue so le laude la gloria e l'honore
Et onne benedictione.
Ad te solo, Altissimo, se confano
Et nullu homo ene dignu te mentovare.

Laudato sie, mi Signore; cun tutte le tue creature
Spetialmente messor lo frate sole
Lo qual jorna et allumini noi per loi.
Et ellu è bellu e radiante cun grande splendore
De te, Altissimo, porta significatione.

Laudato si', mi Signore, per sora luna e le stelle,
In celu l'ai formate clarite et pretiose et belle.

Laudato si', mi Signore, per frate vento
Et per aere et nubilo et sereno et onne tempo,
Per lo quale a le tue creature dai sustentamento.

Laudato si', mi Signore, per sor'aqua
La quale è multo utile et humile et pretiosa et casta . . .

Laudato si', mi Signore, per sora nostra morte corporale
Da la quale nullu homo vivente po scappare,
Guai a quelli che morranno ne le peccata mortali,
Beati quelli che trovarà ne le tue sanctissime voluntati
Ca la morte secunda nol farrà male.

Laudate et benedicete mi Signore et ringratiate
Et serviteli cun grande humilitate.

SAN FRANCESCO D'ASSISI

Sonnet

If I were fire, I'd burn the world away;
If I were wind, I'd turn my storms thereon;
If I were water, I'd soon let it drown;
If I were God, I'd sink it from the day;

If I were Pope, I'd never feel quite gay
Until there was no peace beneath the sun;
If I were Emperor, what would I have done? —
I'd lop men's heads all 'round in my own way.

If I were Death, I'd look my father up;
If I were Life, I'd run away from him;
And I'd treat my mother to like calls and runs.

If I were Cecco (and that's all my hope),
I'd pick the nicest girls to suit my whim,
And other folk should get the ugly ones.

Translated by D. G. Rossetti

Cecco Angiolieri (c. 1260-1312), the antithesis of the religious and of the Dolce stil nuovo (Sweet New Style) poets who idealized woman, vents his feelings in humorous, lusty, picturesque vernacular, reflecting his dim view of the world as in this sonnet. He throws barbs particularly at his father for his parsimony in doling out his allowance.

S'i' fossi foco, arderei lo mondo;
S'i' fossi vento, lo tempesterei;
S'i' fossi acqua, io l' annegherei;
S'i' fossi Dio, mandereil' n profondo;

S'i' fossi papa, sare' allor giocondo
Che tutt' i cristian tribolerei;
S'i' fossi 'imperator, sai che farei?
A tutti mozzarei lo capo a tondo.

S'i' fossi morte, andarei da mio padre;
S'i' fossi vita, fuggirei da lui:
Similemente faria di mi' madre.

S'i' fossi Cecco, com' i' sono e fui,
Torrei le donne giovanni e leggiadre,
E vecchie e laide lasserei altrui.

CECCO ANGIOLIERI

Beatrice

My lady looks so gentle and so pure
When yielding salutation by the way,
That the tongue trembles and has nought to say,
And the eyes, which fain would see, may not endure.

And still, amid the praise she hears secure,
She walks with humbleness for her array;
Seeming a creature sent from Heaven to stay
On earth, and show a miracle made sure.

She is so pleasant in the eyes of men
That through the sight the inmost heart doth gain
A sweetness which needs proof to know it by:

And from between her lips there seems to move
A soothing spirit that is full of love,
Saying forever to the soul, "O sigh!"

Translated by D. G. ROSSETTI

Dante Alighieri (1265-1321) is best known for his immortal Divine Comedy, an allegorical voyage through hell, purgatory and heaven, written in 100 cantos. Dante is guided through hell and purgatory by the Roman poet Virgil, and through heaven by Beatrice, his life-long love, a love more spiritual and philosophical than physical. His collection of poems expressing his love for her, La vita nuova (The New Life), from which the above sonnet is taken, praises Beatrice as a reflection of God's glory and an inspiration to achieve eternal beatitude. Dante is the outstanding poet of the Dolce stil nuovo.

Tanto gentile e tanto onesta pare
La donna mia quand'ella altrui saluta,
Ch'ogni lingua divien tremando muta
E gli occhi non l'ardiscon di guardare.

Ella si va, sentendosi laudare,
Benignamente d'umiltà vestuta
E par che sia una cosa venuta
Da cielo in terra a miracol mostrare.

Mostrasi sì piacente a chi la mira
Che dà per gli occhi una dolcezza al core
Che intender non la può chi non la prova :

E par che da la sua labbia si mova
Un spirito soave pien d'amore,
Che va dicendo a l'anima : — Sospira.

DANTE ALIGHIERI

THROUGH ME THE WAY IS TO THE WOEFUL CITY;
  THROUGH ME THE WAY UNTO ETERNAL PAIN;
  THROUGH ME THE WAY AMONG THOSE DEAD TO PITY.
JUSTICE MY MAKER MOVED WHO RULES ABOVE;
  THERE CAME UNTO MY MAKING POWER DIVINE,
  WISDOM PREEMINENT AND PRIMAL LOVE.
BEFORE I WAS, NO THINGS CREATED WERE,
  UNLESS ETERNAL; ETERNAL I ENDURE.
  LEAVE YE ALL HOPE BEHIND WHO ENTER HERE.
I saw these words, colored so cloudily,
  Engraven above the archway of a gate.
  "Master," I said, "their sense is hard to me."
And he, as one acquainted with the place:
  "Here must thou do away with all mistrust;
  Let die in thee whatever fear is base.
We come now to the place where I have said
  Thou shouldst behold the hapless folk by whom
  The true good of the mind is forfeited."
And thereupon he took my hand in his
  With look so kind that I was comforted,
  And drew me in among the mysteries.
Here sighs and clamors and shrill wailings burst
  Loud echoing upon the starless air;
  Whereby to weeping was I moved at first:
Uncouth tongues, utterances horrible,
  Words of despondency and tones of wrath,
  High voices and hoarse, and sounds of hands as well,
Made up a tumult, which so swirling goes
  Forever in that air of timeless murk
  As sand in deserts when a whirlwind blows.
And I, who felt my brow with horror bound,
  Cried out: "What is this, Master, that I hear?
  What is this folk whom sorrows so confound?"

PER ME SI VA NELLA CITTA DOLENTE,
  PER ME SI VA NELL'ETERNO DOLORE,
  PER ME SI VA TRA LA PERDUTA GENTE.
GIUSTIZIA MOSSE IL MIO ALTO FATTORE,
  FECEMI LA DIVINA POTESTATE,
  LA SOMMA SAPIENZA E IL PRIMO AMORE.
DINANZI A ME NON FUR COSE CREATE,
  SE NON ETERNE; ED IO ETERNO DURO
  LASCIATE OGNI SPERANZA VOI CH'ENTRATE!
Queste parole di colore oscuro
  Vid'io scritte al sommo d'una porta;
  Perch'io: "Maestro, il senso lor m'è duro."
Ed egli a me, come persona accorta:
  "Qui si convien lasciare ogni sospetto,
  Ogni viltà convien che qui sia morta.
Noi siam venuti al luogo ov'io t'ho detto
  Che tu verdrai le genti dolorose
  Ch'anno perduto il ben dello intelletto."
E poi che la sua mano alla mia pose
  Con lieto volto, ond'io mi confortai,
  Mi mise dentro alle segrete cose.
Quivi, sospiri, pianti ed alti guai
  Risonavan per l'aer senza stelle,
  Perch'io al cominciar ne lagrimai.
Diverse lingue, orribili favelle,
  Parole di dolore, accenti d'ira,
  Voci alte e fioche, e suon di man con elle,
Facevano un tumulto, il qual s'aggira
  Sempre in quell'aria senza tempo tinta,
  Come la rena quando a turbo spira.
Ed io, ch'avea d'orror la testa cinta,
  Dissi: "Maestro, che è quel ch'io odo?
  E che gente è, che par nel duol si vinta?"

And he to me: "These miserable ways
   They hold, the most unhappy souls of those
   Who lived without disgrace and without praise.
Commingled are they with that caitiff choir
   Of angels who rebelled not, yet to God
   Were faithless; all for self was their desire.
Heaven refuses them, lest they should stain
   Its glory; and deep hell admits them not,
   Lest even the damned from them some glory gain."
And I: "Master, what weighs so heavily
   Upon them that thus loudly they lament?"
   He answered: "Briefly I will tell it thee.
These have not hope of death; yet odious
   Is so their blinded life that any lot,
   Be it but other, leaves them envious.
Their fame on earth is as a breath on glass;
   Mercy and justice hold them in disdain;
   Let us not speak of them, but look and pass."
And I beheld a banner as I looked,
   That ever ran in circles rapidly,
   As if no instant of repose it brooked;
And such a train of people followed on
   Behind it, that I hardly had believed
   So many death already had undone.

Translated by J. B. FLETCHER

This excerpt from Canto III *of* Hell *treats of the damned who were too weak-willed to do either good or evil. The selection is characteristic of the terse, vigorous, unrestrained descriptions in the* Inferno.

Ed egli a me: "Questo misero modo
    Tengon l'anime triste di coloro
    Che visser senza infamia e senza lodo.
Mischiate sono a quel cattivo coro
    Degli angeli che non furon ribelli.
    Nè fur fedeli a Dio, ma per sè foro.
Cacciarli i ciel' per non esser men belli;
    Nè lo profondo inferno gli riceve,
    Che alcuna gloria i rei avrebber d'elli."
Ed io: "Maestro, che è tanto greve
    A lor, che lamentar gli fa sì forte?"
    Rispose: "Dicerolti molto breve.
Questi non hanno speranza di morte,
    E la lor cieca vita è tanto bassa,
    Che invidiosi son d'ogni altra sorte.
Fama di loro il mondo esser non lassa;
    Misericordia e giustizia gli sdegna.
    Non ragioniam di lor ma guarda e passa."
Ed io, che riguardai, vidi un'insegna
    Che girando correva tanto ratta
    Che d'ogni posa mi pareva indegna.
E dietro le venia sì lunga tratta
    Di gente, ch'io non avrei mai creduto
    Che morte tanta n'avesse disfatta.

DANTE ALIGHIERI

As doves, when their desire is calling, fly
> On spread and level wing to the sweet nest,
> Carried by their own will along the sky,

So, issuing from the troop where Dido is,
> Came these through the malignant air to us,
> Such virtue had my gentle urgencies.

"O mortal one, courteous and humane,
> Who through the livid air goest greeting us
> That left upon the world a crimson stain,

Were friend the Ruler of the universe,
> Truly we would entreat him for thy peace
> For having pity on our fault perverse.

Whate'er to hear or say it be thy will,
> That we will hear, and thereof speak to thee,
> The while for us the wind, as now, is still . . .

Love, who on gentle heart at once attends,
> Allured this other with the comely form
> Reft from me, — and the manner still offends.

Love, who none loved not loving will allow,
> Allured me with delight in him so strong
> That, as thou seest, it leaves me not e'en now . . .

When I had heard those spirits sore-betrayed,
> I bowed my face, and kept it lowered so,
> Until — "What ponderest thou?" — the Poet said.

When I made answer, I began: "Alas!
> How many a sweet thought, what great desire
> Led on these spirits to their woeful pass!"

And then to them I turned, and spoke again;
> And I began: Francesca, thine afflictions
> Move me to tears of pity and of pain.

But tell me, in the season of sweet sighing,
> By what and how might love empower you
> To know the longings dimly underlying?"

Quali colombe, dal disio chiamate,
    Con l'ali alzate e ferme al dolce nido
    Vengon per l'aere dal voler portate;
Cotali uscir della schiera ov'è Dido,
    A noi venendo per l'aere maligno,
    Sì forte fu l'affettuoso grido.
"O animal grazioso e benigno
    Che visitando vai per l'aere perso
    Noi che tingemmo il mondo di sanguigno,
Se fosse amico il re dell'universo,
    Noi pregheremmo lui della tua pace,
    Poi c'hai pietà del nostro mal perverso.
Di quel ch'udire e che parlar vi piace,
    Noi udiremo e parleremo a vui,
    Mentre che 'l vento, come fa, si tace . . .
Amor, ch'al cor gentil ratto s'apprende,
    Prese costui della bella persona
    Che mi fu tolta; e 'l modo ancor m'offende.
Amor, ch'a nullo amato amar perdona,
    Mi prese del costui piacer si forte
    Che, come vedi, ancor non m'abbandona . . .
Quand'io intesi quell'anime offense,
    Chinai il viso, e tanto il tenni bassu,
    Fin che il poeta mi disse: "Che pense?"
Quando risposi cominciai: "Oh lasso,
    Quanti dolci pensier, quanto disio
    Menò costoro al doloroso passo!"
Poi mi rivolsi a loro e parlai io,
    E cominciai: "Francesca, i tuoi martiri
    A lacrimar mi fanno tristo e pio.
Ma dimmi: al tempo de' dolci sospiri,
    A che e come concedette amore
    Che conosceste i dubbiosi disiri?"

And she to me: "There is not greater woe
  Than recollection of the happy time
  In wretchedness; and this thy Sage doth know.
But if in thee so great affection seeks
  To see laid bare the first root of our love,
  I can but do as one who weeps and speaks.
For pleasure on a day of Lancelot
  We two were reading, how love mastered him.
  We were alone; misgiving had we not.
And oftentimes that which we read would call
  Our eyes to meeting, and make pale our faces;
  But one part only brought us to our fall.
When we had read there how the longed-for smile
  Was kissed by such a lover, this one then,
  Who parts not from me this eternal while,
Kissed me upon my mouth all tremblingly.
  A Gallehaut was the book, and he who wrote it.
  That day we read no further, I and he."
While to me thus one spirit was replying,
  The other wept so, that for pitying dread
  Faintness came over me as I were dying;
I fell, as falls the body of one dead.

Translated by J. B. FLETCHER

This excerpt from Canto V *of* Hell *tells of Paolo and his sister-in-law Francesca who are condemned to be swept along together eternally through dark winds. Dante's sympathetic account of their illicit but irresistible love raises it to the level of immortality. Francesca speaks to Dante as Virgil listens and Paolo weeps.*

E quella a me: "Nessun maggior dolore
    Che ricordarsi del tempo felice
    Nella miseria; e ciò sa il tuo dottore.
Ma s'a conoscer la prima radice
    Del nostro amor tu hai cotanto affetto
    Dirò come colui che piange e dice.
Noi leggevamo un giorno per diletto
    Di Lancialotto come amor lo strinse:
    Soli eravamo e senza alcun sospetto.
Per più fiate li occhi ci sospinse
    Quella lettura, e scolorocci il viso;
    Ma solo un punto fu quel che ci vinse.
Quando leggemmo il disiato riso
    Esser baciato da cotanto amante
    Questi, che mai da me non fia diviso,
La bocca mi baciò tutto tremante.
    Galeotto fu il libro e chi lo scrisse:
    Quel giorno più non vi leggemmo avante."
Mentre che l'uno spirto questo disse,
    L'altro piangea, sì che di pietate
    Io venni men, così com'io morisse;
E caddi come corpo morto cade.

DANTE ALIGHIERI

Saint Bernard's Prayer

Thou Virgin Mother, daughter of thy Son,
    Humble and high beyond all other creature,
    The limit fixed of the eternal counsel,
Thou art the one who such nobility
    To human nature gave, that its Creator
    Did not disdain to make himself its creature.
Within thy womb rekindled was the love,
    By heat of which in the eternal peace
    After such wise this flower has germinated.
Here unto us thou art a noonday torch
    Of charity, and below there among mortals
    Thou art the living fountain-head of hope.
Lady, thou art so great, and so prevailing,
    That he who wishes grace, nor runs to thee,
    His aspirations without wings would fly.
Not only thy benignity give succor
    To him who asketh it, but oftentimes
    Forerunneth of its own accord the asking.
In thee compassion is, in thee is pity,
    In thee magnificence; in thee unites
    Whate'er of goodness is in any creature . . .

Translated by HENRY W. LONGFELLOW

Saint Bernard, addressing the Virgin Mary in Paradise, where the vast multitude of the blessed is gathered around in the form of an immense rose, begs her to ask God to permit Dante to gaze upon His Divine Presence.

Vergine madre, figlia del tuo figlio
    Umile e alta più che creatura,
    Termine fisso d'eterno consiglio,
Tu se' colei che l'umana natura
    Nobilitasti sì che 'l suo fattore
    Non disdegnò di farsi sua creatura.
Nel ventre tuo si raccese l'amore
    Per lo cui caldo nell'eterna pace
    Così è germinato questo fiore.
Qui se' a noi meridiana face
    Di caritate, e giuso, infra i mortali
    Se' di speranza fontana vivace.
Donna, se' tanto grande e tanto vali,
    Che qual vuol grazia ed a te non ricorre,
    Sua disianza vuol volar senz'ali.
La tua benignità non pur soccorre
    A chi domanda, ma molte fiate
    Liberamente al dimandar precorre.
In te misericordia, in te pietate,
    In te magnificenza, in te s'aduna
    Quantunque in creatura è di bontate.

DANTE ALIGHIERI

Yon nightingale, whose strain so sweetly flows,
Mourning her ravish'd young or much-loved mate,
A soothing charm o'er all the valleys throws
And skies, with notes well tuned to her sad state:

And all the night she seems my kindred woes
With me to weep and on my sorrows wait;
Sorrows that from my own fond fancy rose,
Who deem'd a goddess could not yield to fate.

How easy to deceive who sleeps secure!
Who could have thought that to dull earth would turn
Those eyes that as the sun shone bright and pure?

Ah! now what Fortune wills I see full sure:
That loathing life, yet living I should see
How few its joys, how little they endure!

ANONYMOUS

*Francesco Petrarca (1304-1374) brought together in his cele-
brated* Canzoniere (Collection of Lyrics) *366 sonnets and other
poems, almost all of them centering on his love for Laura before and
after her death. Unlike Beatrice for Dante, Laura was for Petrarch
primarily a real, physical love and in the* Canzoniere *he describes
her actions and his reactions in analytical, artistic, lyrical detail.
Frequently the things of nature reflect the poet's emotional state, as
in the above sonnet the nightingale recalls the sorrow of Laura's
passing.*

Quel rosigniuol che sì soave piagne,
Forse suoi figli, o sua cara consorte,
Di dolcezza empie il cielo e le campagne
Con tante note sì pietose e scorte;

E tutta notte par che m'accompagne,
E mi rammente la mia dura sorte;
Ch'altri che me non ho di ch' i' mi lagne;
Che 'n dee non credev' io regnasse Morte.

Or cognosco io che mia fera ventura
Vuol che vivendo e lagrimando impari
Come nulla qua giù diletta, e dura.

O che lieve è ingannar chi s'assecura!
Que' duo bei lumi assai più che 'l sol chiari
Chi pensò mai veder far terra oscura!

FRANCESCO PETRARCA

Clear, fresh, and dulcet streams,
Which the fair shape, who seems
To me sole woman, haunted at noon-tide;
Fair bough, so gently fit,
(I sigh to think of it)
Which lent a pillar to her lovely side;
And turf, and flowers bright-eyed,
O'er which her folded gown
Flowed like an angel's down:
And you, O holy air and hushed,
Where first my heart at her sweet glances gushed;
Give ear, give ear, with one consenting,
To my last words, my last and my lamenting.
If 'tis my fate below,
And heaven will have it so,
That Love must close these dying eyes in tears,
May my poor dust be laid
In middle of your shade,
While my soul, naked, mounts to its own spheres . . .
Perhaps, some future hour,
To her accustomed bower
Might come the untamed, and yet the gentle she;
And where she saw me first,
Might turn with eyes athirst
And kinder joy to look again for me;
Then, oh! the charity!
Seeing amidst the stones
The earth that held my bones,
A sigh for very love at last
Might ask of Heaven to pardon me the past:
And Heaven itself could not say nay,
As with her gentle veil she wiped the tears away.
How well I call to mind,
When from those boughs the wind
Shook down upon her bosom flower on flower;

Chiare, fresche, e dolci acque,
Ove le belle membra
Pose colei che sola a me par donna;
Gentil ramo, ove piacque
(Con sospir mi remembra)
A lei di fare al bel fianco colonna;
Erba e fior, che la gonna
Leggiadra ricoverse
Co l' angelico seno;
Aere sacro, sereno,
Ove Amor co' begli occhi il cor m' aperse;
Date udienzia insieme
A le dolenti mie parole estreme.
S'egli è pur mio destino
(E 'l cielo in cio s' adopra)
Che Amor quest' occhi lagrimando chiuda,
Qualche grazia il meschino
Corpo fra voi ricopra,
E torni l' alma al proprio albergo ignuda . . .
Tempo verrà ancor forse
Ch' a l'usato soggiorno
Torni la fera bella e mansueta,
E là 'v' ella mi scorse
Nel benedetto giorno,
Volga la vista disiosa e lieta,
Cercandomi; et, o pieta!
Già terra in fra le pietre
Vedendo, Amor l' inspiri
In guisa che sospira
Sì dolcemente che mercè m' impetre,
E faccia forza al cielo,
Asciugandosi gli occhi col bel velo.
Da' be' rami scendea
(Dolce ne la memoria)
Una pioggia de fior sovra 'l suo grembo;

And there she sat, meek-eyed,
In midst of all that pride,
Sprinkled and blushing through an amorous shower:
Some to her hair paid dower
And seemed to dress the curls,
Queenlike, with gold and pearls;
Some, snowing on her drapery stopped,
Some on the earth, some on the water dropped;
While others, fluttering from above,
Seemed wheeling round in pomp, and saying, "Here reigns Love."
How often then I said,
Inward, and filled with dread,
"Doubtless this creature came from Paradise!"
For at her look the while,
Her voice, and her sweet smile,
And heavenly air, truth parted from mine eyes;
So that, with long-drawn sighs,
I said, as far from men,
"How came I here, and when?"
I had forgotten; and alas!
Fancied myself in heaven, not where I was;
And from that time till this, I bear
Such love for the green bower, I cannot rest elsewhere.

Translated by LEIGH HUNT

One day Petrarch saw Laura basking in the sun on the bank of a river and was moved to compose this famous Canzone (Song), *from which only eleven lines have been omitted. The poet, knowing the espoused Laura is out of reach, finds solace instead in the things which surround her.*

Et ella si sedea
Umile in tanta gloria,
Coverta già de l' amoroso nembo :
Qual fior cadea sul lembo,
Qual su le treccie bionde,
Ch' oro forbito e perle
Eran quel dì a vederle ;
Qual si posava in terra, e qual su l' onde ;
Qual con un vago errore
Girando parea dir — qui regna Amore.
Quante volte diss' io
Allor pien di spavento :
— Costei per fermo nacque in paradiso ! —
Così carco d' oblio
Il divin portamento,
E 'l volto, e le parole, e 'l dolce riso,
M' aveano e sì diviso
Da l' imagine vera,
Ch' i' dicea sospirando :
— Qui come venn' io, o quando ? —
Credendo esser in ciel, non là dov' era.
Da indi in qua mi piace
Questa erba sì, ch' altrove non ho pace.

FRANCESCO PETRARCA

Mensola's Metamorphosis

Then Diana began to call out
To her with piercing cries:
"Mensola, do not escape, for you cannot.
If I wish it, you shall not cross the river . . ."

In spite of this Mensola did not check her flight;
Instead she ran headlong down the slope.
And on reaching the river waded in
To ford it. But Diana pronounced
Certain magic words and, addressing them to the river,
Commanded that it retain Mensola.

The hapless girl was already in mid-stream
When she felt a numbness in her limbs.
And then and there, as it pleased Diana,
Mensola began to turn to water.
And from that time hence that river bore
Her name, as it does to this very day . . .

The nymphs who stood with Diana, on seeing
How Mensola had been dissolved into water
And how she flowed as one with the river,
Because they loved her dearly from the first,
With pity and tears all remarked:
"Oh, wretched, luckless companion,
What sin was yours as to condemn you
To flow like water in wave after wave?"

Translated by A. M. D.

Giovanni Boccaccio (1313-1375), world renowned for his prose masterpiece, The Decameron, *also composed great narrative poems. In this episode from the* Ninfale Fiesolano *the goddess Diana employs her magical powers to punish the nymph, Mensola, who had indiscreetly violated Diana's strict prohibition against love-making.*

Diana incominciò allotta a dire
Inverso lei, con grandissime gride:
"Mensola, non fuggir, chè non potrai,
Se io vorrò, nè 'l fiume passerai!..."

Mensola già per questo non ristette,
Ma fugge quanto può alla pendice;
E giunt' al fiume dentro vi si mette
Per valicarlo; ma Diana dice
Certe parole ed al fiume le manda,
E che ritenga Mensola comanda.

La sventurata era già a mezzo l' acque
Quand' ella il piè venir men si sentia;
E quivi, sì come a Diana piacque,
Mensola in acqua allor si convertia
E sempre poi in quel fiume si giacque
Il nome suo, ed ancor tuttavia...

Le ninfe ch' en con Diana, veggendo
Come Mensola er acqua diventata
E giù per lo gran fiume va correndo,
Perchè molto l' avean in prim' amata,
Per pietà tutte dicevan piangendo:
"O misera compagna sventurata,
Qual peccato fu quel che t' ha condotta
A correr sì com' acqua a fiotta a fiotta?"

GIOVANNI BOCCACCIO

The Triumph of Bacchus and Ariadne

How wonderful is youth,
That flies so quickly by!
He who wishes to be gay, let him.
For tomorrow brings no certainty.

Here are Bacchus and Ariadne;
Beautiful are they and deep in love.
Since time is fleeting and deceiving,
Forever are they in happy company . . .

These happy little satyrs
Of the nymphs enamored,
In every cavern and woodland
Have set snares for them by the hundred.
Now, by Bacchus inebriated,
Dance and gambol endlessly.
He who wishes to be gay, let him;
For tomorrow brings no certainty.

These nymphs even pleasure take
In being startled by them.
By Love none can be spared,
Unless he crude and loathsome be.
Now, all commingled,
They make music and sing continually.
He who wishes to be gay, let him;
For tomorrow brings no certainty.

Translated by A. M. D.

Lorenzo de' Medici (1449-1492), called the "Magnificent," was ruler of Florence in the most glorious period of the Italian Renaissance. He was also an accomplished poet and wrote songs with which he entertained the populace on festive days. We present here the first four stanzas of one that is suffused with the pleasure-loving pagan spirit of the age.

Quant' è bella giovinezza,
Che si fugge tuttavia!
Chi vuol esser lieto, sia:
Di doman non c'è certezza.

"Quest' è Bacco e Arianna,
Belli, e l'un dell'altro ardenti:
Perchè 'l tempo fugge e inganna,
Sempre insieme stan, contenti . . .

Questi lieti satiretti,
Delle ninfe innamorati
Per caverne e per boschetti
Han lor posto cento agguati:
Or, da Bacco riscaldati,
Ballon salton tuttavia.
Chi vuol esser lieto, sia:
Di doman non c'è certezza.

"Queste ninfe hanno anco caro
Da lor essere ingannate;
Non può fare a Amor riparo
Se non gente rozze e ingrate;
Ora, insieme mescolate,
Suonon, canton tuttavia.
Chi vuol esser lieto, sia:
Di doman non c'è certezza.

LORENZO DE' MEDICI

The Dance-Song of the Roses

I went a-roaming, maidens, one bright day,
In a green garden in mid-month of May.
Violets and lilies grew on every side
Mid the green grass, and young flowers wonderful,
Golden and white and red and azure-eyed;
Toward which I stretched my hands, eager to pull
Plenty to make my fair curls beautiful,
To crown my rippling curls with garlands gay.

I went a-roaming, maidens, one bright day . . .
But when my lap was full of flowers, I spied
Roses at last, roses of every hue;
Therefore I ran to pluck their ruddy pride
Because their perfume was so sweet and true
That all my soul went forth with pleasure new,
With yearning and desire too soft to say.

I went a-roaming, maidens, one bright day . . .
I gazed and gazed. Hard task it were to tell
How lovely were the roses in that hour;
One was but peeping from her verdant shell,
And some were faded, some were scarce in flower.
Then Love said: Go, pluck from the blooming bower
Those that thou seest ripe upon the spray.

I went a-roaming, maidens, one bright day —
In a green garden in mid-month of May . . .

Translated by J. A. SYMONDS

Angelo Poliziano (1454-1494), a member of the court of Lorenzo the Magnificent, has frequently been considered the most exquisite poet of the Italian Renaissance. This fresh, gay dance-song La ballata delle rose (The Dance-Song of the Roses) *is typical of Poliziano's poems. We present it slightly abridged.*

I' mi trovai, fanciulle, un bel mattino
Di mezzo maggio in un verde giardino.
Eran d'intorno violette e gigli
Fra l'erba verde, e vaghi fior novelli
Azzurri gialli candidi e vermigli:
Ond'io porsi la mano a cor di quelli
Per adornar e' mie' biondi capelli
E cinger di grillanda el vago crino.

I' mi trovai, fanciulle, un bel mattino . . .
Ma poi ch' i' ebbi pien di fiori un lembo,
Vidi le rose e non pur d'un colore:
Io corsi allor per empier tutto el grembo,
Perch'era sì soave il loro odore
Che tutto mi senti' destar el core
Di dolce voglia e d'un piacer divino.

I' mi trovai, fanciulle, un bel mattino . . .
I' posi mente: quelle rose allora
Mai non vi potre' dir quant'eran belle:
Quale scoppiava della boccia ancora;
Qual erano un po' passe e qual novelle.
Amor disse allor: — Va', co' di quelle
Che più vedi fiorite in su lo spino. —

I' mi trovai, fanciulle, un bel mattino
Di mezzo maggio in un verde giardino . . .

ANGELO POLIZANO

Morgante and the Boars

And lo! a monstrous herd of swine appears
And onward rushes with tempestuous tread,
And to the fountain's brink precisely pours;
So that the Giant's joined by all the boars.

Morgante at a venture shot an arrow,
Which pierced a pig precisely in the ear,
And passed unto the other side quite through;
So that the boar, defunct, lay tripped up near.
Another, to revenge his fellow farrow,
Against the Giant rushed in fierce career,
And reached the passage with so swift a foot,
Morgante was not now in time to shoot.

Perceiving that the pig was on him close,
He gave him such a punch upon the head,
As floored him so that he no more arose,
Smashing the very bone; and he fell dead
Next to the other. Having seen such blows,
The other pigs along the valley fled;
Morgante on his neck the bucket took,
Full from the spring,
        which neither swerved nor shook . . .

Orlando, seeing him so soon appear
With the dead boars, and with that brimful vase,
Marvelled to see his strength so very great;
So did the abbot, and set wide the gate.

Translated by LORD BYRON

Luigi Pulci (1432-1484), in his epic poem Il Morgante (Morgante), treats of the adventures of Orlando (Roland) from his banishment by Charlemagne to his and Charlemagne's deaths. A comic note dominates the kaleidoscopic story, told in twenty-eight cantos. In this selection from Canto I Orlando sends his squire, the giant Morgante, for water with unexpectedly happy results.

Ecco apparir una gran gregge, al passo,
Di porci, e vanno con molta tempesta,
Ed arrivorno alla fontana appunto,
Donde il gigante è da lor sopraggiunto.

Morgante alla ventura a un saetta:
Appunto nell'orecchio lo 'ncartava;
Dall'altro lato passò la verretta,
Onde 'l cinghial giù morto gambettava;
Un altro, quasi per farne vendetta,
Addosso al gran gigante irato andava;
E perchè e' giunse troppo tosto al varco,
Non fu Morgante a tempo a trar coll'arco.

Vedendosi venuto il porco addosso,
Gli dette in sulla testa un gran punzone,
Per modo che gl' infranse insino all'osso,
E morto allato a quell'altro lo pone;
Gli altri porci, veggendo quel percosso
Si misson tutti in fuga pel vallone;
Morgante si levò il tinello in collo
Ch'era pien d'acqua,
        e non si muove un crollo . . .

Orlando, che 'l vedea tornar sì tosto
Co' porci morti e con quel vaso pieno,
Maravigliossi che sia tanto forte;
Così l'abate; e spalancan le porte.

LUIGI PULCI

Close to Death

The course of my long life hath reached at last,
In fragile bark o'er a tempestuous sea,
The common harbor where must rendered be
Account of all the actions of the past.

The impassioned phantasy, that vague and vast,
Made art an idol and a king to me,
Was an illusion, and but vanity
Were the desires that lured me and harassed.

The dreams of love, that were so sweet of yore,
What are they now, when two deaths may be mine,
One sure, and one forecasting its alarms?

Painting and sculpture satisfy no more.
The soul now turning to the Love Divine,
That oped, to embrace us, on the cross its arms.

Translated by HENRY W. LONGFELLOW

The Sculpture of Night in the Medici Chapels

Sleep is dear to me, but more to be of stone.
As long as wrong and infamy persevere,
It is my great fortune not to see nor hear.
Hence, wake me not, pray! But speak in a soft tone.

Translated by A. M. D.

Michelangelo Buonarroti (1475-1564), the titanic creator of some of the greatest masterpieces of sculpture and painting known to man, was also a great poet. His verse expresses his own anguished conscience and the troubled condition of man in the waning years of the Renaissance. Representative of this are the above sonnet and the epigram.

Giuntò è già 'l corso della vita mia
Con tempestoso mar, per fragil barca,
Al comun porto, ov'a render si varca
Conto e ragion d'ogni opra trista e pia.

Onde l' affettuosa fantasia,
Che l'arte mi fece idol e monarca
Conosco or ben, com'era d'error carca,
E quel ch'a suo mal grado ogn'uom desia.

Gli amorosi pensier, già vani e lieti,
Che fien or, s'a duo morte m'avvicino?
D'una so 'l certo, e l'altra mi minaccia.

Nè pinger nè scolpir fia più che quieti
L'anima volta a quell'amor divino
Ch'aperse a prender noi 'n croce le braccia.

MICHELANGELO BUONARROTI

La Notte delle Cappelle Medicee

Caro m'è 'l sonno e più l'esser di sasso,
Mentre che 'l danno e la vergogna dura.
Non veder, non sentir m'è gran ventura;
Però non mi destar, deh! parla basso.

MICHELANGELO BUONARROTI

The House of Sleep

In blest Arabia lies a pleasant vale,
Removed from village and from city's reach.
By two fair hills o'ershadowed is the dale,
And full of ancient fir and sturdy beech.
Thither the circling sun without avail
Conveys the cheerful daylight: for no breach
The rays can make through boughs spread thickly round;
And it is here a cave runs under ground.

Beneath the shadow of this forest deep,
Into the rock there runs a grotto wide.
Here wildly wandering, ivy-suckers creep,
About the cavern's entrance multiplied.
Harboured within this grot lies heavy Sleep.
Ease, corpulent and gross, upon *this* side,
Upon *that*, Sloth, on earth has made her seat;
Who cannot go, and hardly keeps her feet.

Mindless Oblivion at the gate is found,
Who lets none enter, and agnizes none;
Nor message hears or bears, and from that ground
Without distinction chases every one;
While Silence plays the scout and walks his round,
Equipt with shoes of felt and mantle brown,
And motions from a distance all who meet
Him on his circuit, from the dim retreat.

Translated by W. S. Rose

Ludovico Ariosto (1474-1533), is known principally for his chivalric poem Orlando Furioso (Mad Roland), *one of the most significant and popular works of Italian literature. It has a vast array of characters and episodes in its forty-six cantos. In this selection from* Canto XIV, *the angel Gabriel looks for Silence in order to command him to aid the besieged Charlemagne. He finds him at last in* La casa del sonno (The House of Sleep), *beautifully described here.*

Giace in Arabia una valletta amena,
Lontana da cittadi e da villaggi,
Ch'all'ombra di due monti e tutta piena
D'antiqui abeti e di robusti faggi.
Il Sole indarno il chiaro dì vi mena;
Che non vi può mai penetrar coi raggi,
Sì gli è la via da folti rami tronca:
E quivi entra sotterra una spelonca.

Sotto la negra selva una capace
E spaziosa grotta entra nel sasso,
Di cui la fronte l'edera seguace
Tutta aggirando va con storto passo.
In questo albergo il grave Sonno giace;
L'Ozio da un canto corpulento e grasso,
Da l'altro la Pigrizia in terra siede,
Che non può andare, e mal reggesi in piede.

Lo smemorato Oblio sta sulla porta;
Non lascia entrar nè riconosce alcuno:
Non ascolta imbasciata, nè riporta;
E parimente tien cacciato ognuno.
Il Silenzio va intorno, e fa la scorta:
Ha le scarpe di feltro e 'l mantel bruno:
Ed a quanti n'incontra, di lontano
Che non debban venir cenna con mano.

Ludovico Ariosto

In a hundred knots, amid those green abodes,
In a hundred parts, their cyphered names are dight;
Whose many letters are so many goads,
Which Love has in his bleeding heart-core pight.
He would discredit in a thousand modes,
That which he credits in his own despite;
And would parforce persuade himself, *that* rhind
Other Angelica than his had signed.

"And yet I know these characters," he cried,
"Of which I have so many read and seen;
By her may this Medoro be belied,
And me, she, figured in the name, may mean." . . .

Here from his horse the sorrowing County lit,
And at the entrance of the grot surveyed
A cloud of words, which seemed but newly writ,
And which the young Medoro's hand had made . . .

"Gay plants, green herbage, rill of limpid vein,
And, grateful with cool shade, thou gloomy cave,
Whereoft, by many wooed with fruitless pain,
Beauteous Angelica, the child of grave
King Galaphron, within my arms has lain;
For the convenient harbourage you gave,
I, poor Medoro, can but in my lays,
As recompence, forever sing your praise . . ."

Three times, and four, and six, the lines imprest
Upon the stone that wretch perused, in vain
Seeking another sense than was exprest,
And ever saw the thing more clear and plain;
And all the while, within his troubled breast,
He felt an icy hand his heart-core strain.
With mind and eyes close fastened on the block,
At length he stood, not differing from the rock . . .

Angelica e Medor con cento nodi
Legati insieme, e in cento lochi vede.
Quante lettere son, tanti son chiodi
Coi quali Amore il cor gli punge e fiede.
Va col pensier carcando in mille modi
Non creder quel ch'al suo dispetto crede:
Ch'altra Angelica sia, creder si sforza
Ch'abbia scritto il suo nome in quella scorza.

Poi dice: "Conosco io pur queste note:
Di tal' io n'ho tante vedute e lette.
Finger questo Medoro ella si puote:
Forse ch'a me questo cognome mette . . ."

Il mesto Conte a piè quivi discese;
E vide in su l'entrata della grotta
Parole assai, che di sua man distese
Medoro avea, che parean scritte allotta . . .

"Liete piante, verdi erbe, limpide acque,
Spelonca opaca e di fredde ombre grata,
Dove la bella Angelica che nacque
Di Galafron, da molti invano amata,
Spesso nelle mie braccia nuda giacque:
Della comodità che qui m'è data,
Io povero Medor ricompensarvi
D'altro non posso che d'ognor lodarvi: . . ."

Tre volte e quattro e sei lesse lo scritto
Quello infelice, e pur cercando in vano
Che non vi fosse quel che v'era scritto;
E sempre lo vedea più charo e piano:
Ed ogni volta in mezzo il petto afflitto
Stringersi il cor sentia con fredda mano.
Rimase al fin con gli occhi e con la mente
Fissi nel sasso, al sasso indifferente . . .

All night about the forest roved the count,
And, at the break of daily light, was brought
By his unhappy fortune to the fount,
Where his inscription young Medoro wrought.
To see his wrongs inscribed upon that mount,
Inflamed his fury so, in him was nought
But turned to hatred, frenzy, rage, and spite;
Nor paused he more, but bared his faulchion bright.

Cleft through the writing; and the solid block,
Into the sky, in tiny fragments sped.
Wo worth each sapling and that caverned rock,
Where Medore and Angelica were read!
So scathed, that they to shepherd or to flock
Thenceforth shall never furnish shade or bed.
And that sweet fountain, late so clear and pure,
From such tempestuous wrath was ill secure . . .

Here was his helmet, there his shield bestowed;
His arms far off, and, farther than the rest,
His cuirass; through the greenwood wide was strowed
All his good gear, in fine; and next his vest
He rent; and, in his fury, naked showed
His shaggy paunch, and all his back and breast.
And 'gan that frenzy act, so passing dread,
Of stranger folly never shall be said.

Translated by W. S. Rose

This selection from Canto XXIII *of* Orlando Furioso *recounts in vivid detail the incredulity, mounting fury, and subsequent madness of Orlando on discovering that his great love, Angelica, has fallen in love with a Saracen soldier, Medoro.*

Pel bosco errò tutta la notte il Conte;
E allo spuntar della diurna fiamma
Lo tornò il suo destin sopra la fonte,
Dove Medoro isculse l'epigramma.
Veder l'ingiuria sua scritta nel monte
L'accese sì, ch'in lui non restò dramma
Che non fosse odio, rabbia, ira e furore;
Nè più indugiò, che trasse il brando fuore.

Tagliò lo scritto e 'l sasso e sino al cielo
A volo alzar fè le minute schegge.
Infelice quell'antro, ed ogni stelo
In cui Medoro e Angelica si legge!
Così restar quel dì, ch'ombra nè gelo
A pastor mai non daran più, nè a gregge:
E quella fonte, già sì chiara e pura,
Da contanta ira fu poco sicura; . . .

Qui riman l'elmo, e là riman lo scudo;
Lontan gli arnesi, e più lontan l'usbergo;
L'arme sue tutte, in somma vi concludo,
Avean pel bosco differente albergo
E poi si squarciò i panni, e mostrò ignudo
L'ispido ventre, e tutto 'l petto e 'l tergo;
E cominciò la gran follia, sì orrenda,
Che della più non sarà mai chi 'ntenda.

LUDOVICO ARIOSTO

Bliss of Love

I do not envy you one bit, holy angels,
For all your glory and all your blessings,
And all those ardent desires fulfilled
Merely by standing before the Lord on High;

For my delights are such and so many,
That they cannot fit in earthly heart,
When before me I have the serene life-giving eyes
Of the one who constrains me to write and sing ever more.

And just as in heaven great refreshment and life
You are wont to gather from His divine image,
So do I here on earth from his infinite beauty.

Only in this do you surpass my joy:
Yours is eternal and immutable,
My bliss can quickly vanish.

Translated by W. G.

Gaspara Stampa (1523-1554) is perhaps the best of the female poets of the Renaissance. Her finest poetry centers on Count Collaltino di Collalto, the great love of her life, who later abandoned her. A melancholy yearning for her lost love pervades most of her poems. Even in this joyful sonnet she ends on a pessimistic note.

Io non v'invidio punto, angeli santi,
Le vostre tante glorie e tanti beni,
E que' disir di ciò che braman pieni,
Stando voi sempre a l'alto Sire avanti;

Perchè i diletti miei son tali e tanti,
Che non posson capire in cor terreni
Mentr' ho davanti i lumi almi e sereni
Di cui conven che sempre scriva e canti.

E come in ciel gran refrigerio e vita
Dal volto Suo solete voi fruire,
Tal io qua giù da la beltà infinita.

In questo sol vincete il mio gioire,
Che la vostra è eterna e stabilita,
E la mia gloria può tosto finire.

GASPARA STAMPA

My Lady's Sweet Voice

On these shores there are
No flowers so crimson
As the lips of my lady,
Nor does the murmur of the summer breeze
Mid fountains and roses and lilies
Surpass her song in sweet melody,
Song which inflames and delights me —
Only our kisses can interrupt you!

To the Duchess of Urbino

In your green years a crimson rose
You seemed, which to the tepid sunrays and gentle breezes
Opens not its breast, but in its tender cup still
Virgin-like retreats with modesty;

Or rather you resembled, for no mortal thing
Can be likened to you, a heavenly aurora
Which adorns the fields with pearls and the mountains with gold
Bright and fresh in a tranquil sky.

Yet now the less tender years take nought from you,
And though you dress more discreetly, even adorned with rich robes,
Youthful beauty can neither surpass nor rival you.

In like manner more lovely is the flower after its petals
Spreads, fragrant, and the sun at mid-day
More than in the morning, gleams and dazzles.

Translations by W. G.

Torquato Tasso (1544-1595) is Italy's outstanding poet in the second half of the sixteenth century. During the latter part of his life he was disturbed by psychological upheavals of a personal and religious nature. His poetry is sensitively lyrical, as will be noted in the above madrigal and sonnet.

Non sono in queste rive
Fiori così vermigli
Come le labbra de la donna mia,
Nè 'l suon de l'aure estive
Fra fonti e rose e gigli
Fa del suo canto più dolce armonia.
Canto che m'ardi e piaci,
T' interrompano solo i nostri baci!

TORQUATO TASSO

Alla Duchessa di Urbino

Ne gli anni acerbi tuoi purpurea rosa
Sembravi tu, ch'a i rai tepidi a l'ora
Non apre 'l sen, ma nel suo verde ancora
Verginella s'asconde e vergognosa;

O piuttosto parei, che mortal cosa
Non s'assomiglia a te, celeste aurora
Che le campagne imperla e i monti indora
Lucida in ciel sereno e rugiadosa.

Or la men verde età nulla a te toglie;
Nè te, benchè negletta, in manto adorno
Giovinetta beltà vince o pareggia.

Così più vago è il fior, poi che le foglie
Spiega odorate, e 'l sol nel mezzo giorno
Via più che nel mattin luce e fiammeggia.

TORQUATO TASSO

The Crusaders Before Jerusalem

Wing'd is each heart, and winged every heel;
They fly, yet notice not how fast they fly;
But by the time the dewless meads reveal
The fervent sun's ascension in the sky,
Lo, towered Jerusalem salutes the eye!
A thousand pointing fingers tell the tale;
"Jerusalem!" a thousand voices cry,
"All hail, Jerusalem!" hill, down, and dale
Catch the glad sounds, and shout, "Jerusalem, all hail!" . . .

To the pure pleasure which that first far view
In their reviving spirits sweetly shed,
Succeeds a deep contrition, feelings new —
Grief touched with awe, affection mixed with dread;
Scarce dare they now upraise the abject head,
Or turn to Zion their desiring eyes,
The chosen city! where Messias bled
Defrauded Death of his long tyrannies,
New clothed his limbs with life, and reassumed the skies!

Low accents, plaintive whispers, groans profound,
Sighs of a people that in gladness grieves,
And melancholy murmurs float around,
Till the sad air a thrilling sound receives,
Like that which sobs amidst the dying leaves,
When with autumnal winds the forest waves;
Or dash of an insurgent sea that heaves
On lonely rocks, or locked in winding caves,
Hoarse through their hollow aisles in wild low cadence raves.

Each, at his Chief's example, lays aside
His scarf and feathered casque, with every gay
And glittering ornament of knightly pride,
And barefoot treads the consecrated way.

Ali ha ciascuno al core ed ali al piede,
Nè del suo ratto andar però s'accorge:
Ma, quando il sol gli aridi campi fiede
Con raggi assai ferventi, e in alto sorge,
Ecco apparir Gierusalem si vede,
Ecco additar Gierusalem si scorge;
Ecco da mille voci unitamente
Gierusalemme salutar si sente . . .

Al gran piacer che quella prima vista
Dolcemente spirò ne l'altrui petto,
Alta contrizion successe, mista
Di timoroso e riverente affetto;
Osano a pena d'inalzar la vista
Ver' la città, di Cristo albergo eletto,
Dove morì, dove sepolto fue,
Dove poi rivestì le membra sue.

Sommessi accenti e tacite parole,
Rotti singulti e flebili sospiri
De la gente ch'in un s'allegra e duole,
Fan che per l'aria un mormorio s'aggiri
Qual ne le folte selve udir si suole,
S'avvien che tra le frondi il vento spiri;
O quale infra gli scogli, o presso a i lidi
Sibila il mar percosso in rauchi stridi.

Nudo ciascun il piè calca il sentiero;
Che l'essempio de' duci ogn'altro move:
Serico fregio o d'or, piuma o cimiero
Superbo, dal suo capo ognun rimove;

Their thoughts, too, suited to their changed array,
Warm tears devout their eyes in showers diffuse —
Tears, that the haughtiest temper might allay;
And yet, as though to weep they did refuse,
Thus to themselves their hearts of hardness they accuse.

"Here, Lord, where currents from thy wounded side
Stained the besprinkled ground with sanguine red,
Should not these two quick springs at least, their tide
In bitter memory of thy passion shed!
And melt'st thou not, my icy heart, where bled
Thy dear Redeemer? still must pity sleep?
My flinty bosom, why so cold and dead?
Break, and with tears the hallowed region steep!
If that thou weep'st not now, for ever shouldst thou weep!

Translated by J. H. WIFFEN

The above selection is from Tasso's masterpiece, the epic poem Gerusalemme liberata (Jerusalem Delivered) *written in 20 cantos, which deals with the last few months of the Crusade under Godfrey of Boulogne. The poet adds many fictitious and romantic episodes to the historical facts. This excerpt from* Canto III *describes the feelings of exhilaration and awe-struck reverence of the Christians when they finally arrive at the gates of Jerusalem.*

Ed insieme del cor l'abito altero
Depone: e calde e pie lagrime piove:
Pur, quasi al pianto abbia la via rinchiusa,
Così parlando ognun sè stesso accusa:

— Dunque, ove tu, Signor di mille rivi
Sanguinosi il terren lasciasti asperso,
D'amaro pianto almen duo fonti vivi
In sì acerba memoria oggi io non verso?
Agghiacciato mio cor che non derivi
Per gli occhi, e stilli in lagrime converso?
Duro mio cor, chè non ti spetri e frangi?
Pianger ben merti ognor, s'ora non piangi. —

TORQUATO TASSO

The Woodland Siren

But more than any other sweet and noble bird,
That may spread with greater charm its wings and song,
The Woodland Siren, the nightingale,
Pours forth its tremulous and ethereal soul
And modulates in such guise its unique style
As to seem master of the feathered throng.
In a thousand ways it varies its song
And transforms into a thousand its only tongue.

What a wondrous thing to listen to this musical prodigy
Who is so plainly heard, but scarcely seen!
How abruptly it interrupts its song, then renews it!
Now holds a note, then distorts it, and alternately makes it thin, and full;
Now murmurs it solemnly, then gives it subtle quality,
Then embarks on a long sweet warbling chain.
And always, whether it disperses its voice or gathers it in,
With equal melody binds and sets it free.

Oh, what precious rhymes, what rhymes of lamentation,
That sensuous little songster composes for declamation . . .

Translated by A. M. D.

In the late sixteenth and throughout the entire seventeenth century Italian poetry was characterized by all kinds of ingenious externalities, calculated to produce startling effects. The label applied to this poetry is "marinism," after its most representative poet, Giovan Battista Marino (1569-1625). From his Adone, a mythological poem containing over forty thousand verses, we have taken two typical selections. The first describes the remarkable song of the nightingale. In the second, Venus, whose drops of blood stain a rose after she is pricked by its thorns, eulogizes its incomparable beauty.

Ma sovr'ogni augellin vago e gentile,
Che più spieghi leggiadro il canto e 'l volo,
Versa il suo spirto tremulo e sottile
La Sirena de' boschi, il rosignuolo;
E tempra in guisa il peregrino stile
Che par maestro de l'alato stuolo.
In mille fogge il suo cantar distingue,
E trasforma una lingua in mille lingue.

Udir musico mostro o meraviglia!
Che s'ode sì ma si discerne apena,
Come or tronca la voce, or la ripiglia,
Or la ferma, or la torce, or scema or piena,
Or la mormora grave, or l'assottiglia,
Or fa di dolci groppi ampia catena,
E sempre, o se la sparge o se l'accoglie,
Con egual melodia la lega e scioglie.

O che vezzose, o che pietose rime
Lascivetto cantor compone e detta!...

GIOVAN BATTISTA MARINO

The Rose

Rose, smile of love, handiwork of heaven,
Rose with my blood made vermilion,
Prize of the world and adornment of nature,
Of the Earth and the Sun virgin daughter,
Of every nymph and shepherd delight and concern,
Glory of the sweet-scented family,
You hold for every beauty the highest trophies,
Above the common herd of flowers sublime Lady.

Like a proud empress on a beautiful throne,
There you sit on your native shore.
A comely and flattering multitude of breezes
Gathers round to pay you court and serve you,
While a band of sharply armed guards
Surrounds and defends you against all harm . . .

Crimson lady of the gardens, pomp of the meadows,
Jewel of spring, light of April,
Of you the Graces and little winged Cupids
Make garlands for their hair and necklaces for their bosoms.
And whenever to their habitual nourishment return
The nimble bees or the gentle zephyrs,
You give them to drink in ruby cups
Juices dewy and crystalline.

Let not the Sun be too arrogant
In his triumph over the minor stars . . .
With your unique and special beauties
You are the splendor of these lands, he of his.
He in his circle, you on your stem,
You a Sun on earth, and he a rose in heaven.

Translated by A. M. D.

Rosa, riso d'Amor, del ciel fattura,
Rosa del sangue mio fatta vermiglia,
Pregio del mondo e fregio di natura,
De la Terra e del Sol vergine figlia,
D'ogni ninfa e pastor delizia e cura,
Onor de l'odorifera famiglia,
Tu tien d'ogni beltà le palme prime,
Sovra il vulgo de' fior Donna sublime.

Quasi in bel trono imperadrice altera
Siedi colà su la native sponda.
Turba d'aure vezzosa e lusinghiera
Ti corteggia d'intorno e ti seconda;
E di guardie pungenti armata schiera
Ti difende per tutto e ti circonda.

Porpora de' giardin, pompa de' prati,
Gemma di primavera, occhio d'aprile,
Di te le Grazie e gli Amoretti alati
Fan ghirlanda a la chioma, al sen monile.
Tu, qualor torna a gli alimenti usati
Ape leggiadra o zeffiro gentile,
Dai lor da bere in tazza di rubini
Rugiadosi licori e cristallini.

Non superbisca ambizioso il Sole
Di trionfar fra le minori stelle . . .
Tu sei con tue bellezze uniche e sole
Splendor di queste piagge, egli di quelle.
Egli nel cerchio suo, tu nel tuo stelo,
Tu Sole in terra, ed egli rosa in cielo.

GIOVAN BATTISTA MARINO

The Smile of a Beautiful Lady

You lovely scarlet roses,
That amid thorns,
At daybreak, fail to open;
But, as Love's servants,
Guard over
Exquisite treasures of pearly teeth;

Pray tell me, precious,
Amorous roses,
Please explain, that if I fix my glance
On your pretty, sensitive, ardent features,
Forthright
You display a winsome smile? . . .

If a pleasant stream, a gentle breeze,
Through leaves of grass
Wanders murmuring by at morningtide;
If a little meadow with flowers
Is bedecked;
We say the earth is smiling . . .

If ever, among crimson flowers,
Among lilies,
Dawn is clad in a golden veil,
And on sapphire wheels
Moves in its circle,
We say the sky is smiling.

It is, indeed, true: the world smiles
When it is happy;
The sky, when it is glad.
It is really true; but none is able
To fashion
An alluring smile quite like you.

Translated by A. M. D.

Gabriello Chiabrera (1552-1638) was a master of clever conceits and metaphors. The roses of which he speaks in the above poem (abridged) are the lips of his lady-love.

Belle rose porporine,
che tra spine
sull'aurora non aprite;
ma, ministre degli Amori,
bei tesori
di bei denti custodite;

Dite, rose preziose,
amorose,
dite, ond'è, che s' io m'affiso
nel bel guardo, vivo, ardente,
voi repente
disciogliete un bel sorriso?...

Se bel rio, se bell'auretta
tra l'erbetta
sul mattin mormorando erra;
se di fiori un praticello
si fa bello;
noi diciam: ride la terra...

Se giammai tra fior vermigli,
se tra gigli
veste l'Alba un aureo velo,
e su rote di zaffiro
move in giro,
noi diciam che ride il cielo.

Ben è ver; quando è giocondo
ride il mondo,
ride il ciel, quando è gioioso;
ben è ver; ma non san poi
come voi
fare un riso grazioso.

GABRIELLO CHIABRERA

Short Arias

I

If every man's internal anguish
On his forehead were easily read
How many of those who inspire envy
Would move us to pity instead!

II

That drop of water that falls abruptly
Down the alpine slope,
Rebounds, shatters and complains,
But limpid it becomes.

Another remains at rest, however,
In the dark shadowy depths,
But in that repose it loses
Its beauty, completely.

III

Though lacking senses
Grateful, too, is the little shrub,
To the friendly stream
Whose moisture it enjoys.

Through it, now adorned with leaves,
Gracefully the shrub gives thanks
When it from the sun defends
Its kindly benefactor.

Translated by W. G.

Pietro Metastasio (1698-1782), great lyric poet, brought to perfection the melodrama (drama with music) of the eighteenth century. Particularly delightful are the ariette *(short arias) in his* melodrammi, *many of which became very popular.*

I

Se a ciascun l' interno affanno
Si leggesse in fronte scritto,
Quanti mai, che invidia fanno,
Ci farebbero pietà!

II

Quell'onda che ruina
Dalla pendice alpina,
Balza, si frange e mormora,
Ma limpida si fa.

Altra riposa, è vero,
In cupo fondo ombroso,
Ma perde in quel riposo
Tutta la sua beltà.

III

Benchè di senso privo,
Fin l'arboscello è grato
A quell'amico rivo,
Da cui riceve umor.

Per lui di frondi ornato
Bella mercè gli rende,
Quando dal sol difende
Il suo benefattor.

PIETRO METASTASIO

Morning

With Dawn the Morning rises, ere the Sun
Above the far horizon big appears,
To wake with joy the life of plain and wave
And beast and herb. Then the good countryman
Quits his dear bed warm'd through the chilly night
By company of faithful spouse and babes;
And shouldering the sacred implements
Ceres and Pales anciently devis'd,
Drives the slow ox before him toward the field;
And as he moves along the narrow path
Stirring the dainty curving boughs he shakes
The dewy drops that glistening refract
Gem-like the young rays of the Sun. Then too
Rises the smith, once more the sounding forge
He opens and again his hand he sets
To works begun, through yesternight unfinish'd;
Whether he labour to secure with key
Of puzzling wards and iron engines strong
The coffer'd wealth of the uneasy rich,
Or cunningly with gold and silver chasing
To ornament such jewell'd toys and vases
As may adorn the bride or deck the table.

But what? The very sound of these my words
Sets thee aquake? Lifts upright on thy head
Hair bristling like the prickly porcupine?
Ah, such is not thy morning Sir, 'tis true;
No frugal meal at sunset didst thou share;
By the uncertain twilight didst not seek
Thy rest in bedding rude and comfortless
As th' humble crowd are still condemn'd to do . . .

Far later were the hours of night prolong'd
By thee among th' assemblies, and the scenes
Of vocal stage, and haunts of poignant play.

Sorge il Mattino in compagnia dell'Alba
Innanzi al Sol, che di poi grande appare
Su l'estremo orizzonte a render lieti
Gli animali e le piante e i campi e l'onde.
Allora il buon villan sorge dal caro
Letto cui la fedel sposa e i minori
Suoi figlioletti intiepidir la notte;
Poi sul collo recando i sacri arnesi
Che prima ritrovar Cerere e Pale,
Va, col bue lento innanzi, al campo, e scuote
Lungo il picciol sentier da' curvi rami
Il rugiadoso umor che, quasi gemma,
I nascenti del Sol raggi rifrange.
Allora sorge il fabbro, e la sonante
Officina riapre, e all'opre torna
L'altro dì non perfette, o se di chiave
Ardua e ferrati ingegni all'inquieto
Ricco l'arche assecura, o se d'argento
E d'oro incider vuol gioielli e vasi
Per ornamento a nuove spose o a mense.

Ma che? tu inorridisci, e mostri in capo
Qual istrice pungente, irti i capelli
Al suon di mie parole? Ah, non è questo,
Signor, il tuo mattin. Tu col cadente
Sol non sedesti a parca mensa, e al lume
Dell'incerto crepuscolo non gisti
Ieri a corcarti in male agiate piume
Come dannato è a far l'umile vulgo . . .

Tu tra le veglie, e le canore scene,
E il patetico gioco oltre più assai
Producesti la notte; e stanco alfine

Tired at last, in golden coach reclining,
With hurrying rattling wheels and crashing din
Of flying horse-hoofs far and wide thou shock'st
The still nocturnal air, . . .

Such thy majestic home-coming; but here
Awaited thee fresh duties at the table
O'erspread with pungent foods, and joyous wines
Grown on the hills of France, of Tuscany,
Of Spain, or glowing in the Hungarian bottle
That Bacchus with green ivy crown'd, and said
Sit there, the tables' queen. Somnus at last
With his own hand shook up the downy bed
That now receiv'd thee, while thy faithful servant
Lower'd the silken curtains, and the note
Of cock-crow sweetly lull'd thee fast asleep
With the same voice that calls the world awake.

Translated by H. M. BOWER

Giuseppe Parini (1729-1799), although educated as a priest, served for many years as tutor in aristocratic families. This experience gave him the inspiration and background for the great satirical poem Il Giorno *(The Day), in which he describes how a young decadent aristocrat squanders his time in profligate activities while he remains totally oblivious to his own corruption. Our selection, extracted from that part of the poem entitled* Il Mattino *(Morning), contrasts the constructive lives of farmers and artisans who rise with the rooster's crow, and the wasteful one of the aristocrat who goes to bed with the same cry.*

In aureo cocchio, col fragor di calde
Precipitose rote e il calpestio
Di volanti corsier, lunge agitasti
Il quieto aere notturno . . .

Così tornasti a la magion; ma quivi
A novi studi ti attendea la mensa
Cui ricoprien pruriginosi cibi
E licor lieti di francesi colli,
O d'ispani, o di toschi, o l'ongarese
Bottiglia a cui di verde edera Bacco
Concedette corona, e disse: siedi
Delle mense reìna. Al fine il Sonno
Ti sprimacciò le morbide coltrici
Di propria mano, ove, te accolto, il fido
Servo calò le seriche cortine:
E a te soavemente i lumi chiuse
Il gallo che li suole aprire altrui.

GIUSEPPE PARINI

Love and Death

I cry your name a thousand times each day;
    But Death alone makes answer in your stead,
    That Death, which calls to me beyond the dread
    Of Styx, where waves of gloom roll on their way.
When in some ancient vaulted temple I stray,
    To seek 'mid tombs the stone of lovers dead,
    A noble pair, swiftly my gaze is led
    There, fixed, as if my eyes in that tomb lay.
And thus constrained by immense grief I cry:
    "Happy are you, confined in such small space,
    Whose peace the faithless world cannot deny!"
Why live in wandering from place to place,
    Parted by endless strife? Better to lie
    Beneath the sod in indivisible embrace.

The Free Man

A man of sentiment, of courage, born free;
    He reveals himself at once by unmistakable signs.
    He boldly tilts, now against corruption, then against tyrants;
    His countenance is bare, but the rest of him is armed.
Though imbued with lofty messages, disdainfully fearless,
    He cloisters himself within his own silence.
    The infamy of others brings a flush to his cheek;
    Nor does he ever seek the company of despots.
He may sometimes yield, but he will not serve the corrupt times.
    He is hated and feared by rulers
    And no less by slavish and ignoble souls.
Conscious of his own purpose, such a man does not deign
    To manifest the wrath that righteously seethes within him;
    His bearing alone is a lesson against servitude.

Translations by A. M. D.

Vittorio Alfieri (1749-1803), Italy's greatest tragedian and an outstanding romantic poet, was also a champion of individual liberty and Italian political freedom in the dawn of the Risorgimento. These two sonnets are strongly characteristic of his art.

Te chiamo a nome il dì ben mille volte;
    Ed in tua vece, Morte a me risponde:
    Morte, che me di là dalle triste onde
    Di Stige appella, in guise orride e molte.
Cerco talor sotto le arcate volte
    D'antico tempio, ove d'avelli abbonde,
    Se alcun par d'alti amanti un sasso asconde,
    E tosto ivi entro le luci ho sepolte:
Sforzato poi da immenso duolo, io grido:
    "Felici, o voi, cui breve spazio serra,
    Cui più non toglie pace il mondo infido!
È vita questa, che in continua guerra
    Meniam disgiunti, d'uno in altro lido?
    Meglio indivisi fia giacer sotterra.

L'uomo libero

Uom di sensi, e di cor, libero nato,
    Fa di sè tosto indubitabil mostra.
    Or co' vizi e i Tiranni ardito ei giostra,
    Ignudo il volto, e tutto il resto armato:
Or pregno, in suo tacer, d'alto dettato,
    Sdegnosamente impavido s'inchiostra;
    L'altrui viltà la di lui guancia innostra;
    Nè visto è mai dei Dominanti a lato.
Cede ei talor, ma ai tempi rei non serve;
    Abborrito e temuto da chi regna,
    Non men che dalle schiave alme proterve.
Conscio a sè di sè stesso, uom tal non degna
    L'ira esalar che pura in cor gli ferve;
    Ma il sol suo aspetto a non servire insegna.

VITTORIO ALFIERI

On the Liberation of Italy

Beautiful Italy, beloved shores,
Once more my eyes will set on you!
Trembling in my breast, frenzied,
My heart is overcome with joy.

Your beauty, which of tears
Always a bitter fountain was,
Of foreigners and cruel lovers
Of you had made a slave.

But false and ephemeral
Shall be the hope of kings:
The garden of nature, no,
Is not for barbarians.

Bonaparte on seeing your peril
From the Libyan sea he flew;
He saw the tears upon your cheeks,
And forth his thunderbolt drew . . .

With hostile blood the wide fields
Of Marengo lukewarm grew,
And at the thunder and flash of cannon
The startled enemy hordes flew.

The plains of Marengo
The enemy tomb he made.
The garden of nature, no,
Is not for barbarians.

Translated by W. G.

In June 1800, to celebrate the re-establishment by Napoleon of the Cisalpine Republic, temporarily overrun by the Austro-Russian armies during Napoleon's Egyptian campaign, the neo-classical poet, Vincenzo Monti (1754-1828), composed this famous patriotic ode. The complete poem contains ninety-two verses.

Bella Italia, amate sponde,
Pur vi torno a riveder!
Trema in petto e si confonde
L'alma oppressa dal piacer.

Tua bellezza, che di pianti
Fonte amara ognor ti fu,
Di stranieri e crudi amanti
T'avea posta in servitù.

Ma bugiarda e mal sicura
La speranza fia de' re:
Il giardino di natura,
No, pei barbari non è.

Bonaparte al tuo periglio
Dal .nar libico volò;
Vide il pianto del tuo ciglio,
E il suo fulmine impugnò . . .

D'ostil sangue i vasti campi
Di Marengo intiepidir,
E de' bronzi ai tuoni ai lampi
L'onde attonite fuggir.

Di Marengo la pianura
Al nemico tomba diè.
Il giardino di natura,
No, pei barbari non è.

VINCENZO MONTI

To Night

Perhaps because of eternal quiescence
You are the image, to me you come so longed-for,
Oh Night! And when they court you happily —
The summer clouds and gentle breezes —

And when from the snowy clouds troubled
And long shadows you cast on the world,
Always you come when beckoned, and into the secret
Paths of my heart softly find your way.

My thoughts you make wander on the road
That leads to eternal nothingness; and thus absorbed,
The wretched hours flee, and with them the swarms

Of cares, mid which they torment themselves and me;
And while I contemplate your peace, sleeps
That tempestuous spirit that within me rages.

Translated by W. G.

Ugo Foscolo (1778-1827), a poet whose noble, patriotic ideals inspired the generation that fought the battles of the Italian Risorgimento, wrote only twelve sonnets, most of them expressing, as in the one above, a sincere feeling of desperate melancholy. Dei Sepolcri (The Sepulchres) containing 295 lines, is considered his best poem. It is a protest against an edict barring cemeteries from cities and regulating tombs and epitaphs. Foscolo defends the right of burial in cities and the free embellishment of tombs, primarily on the grounds that the tombs serve as an inspiration for the living and link them with the dead. In the selected passage, on pages 80-81, as the poet describes the natural beauty of a cemetery, he reveals how closely the living and the dead are bound.

Forse perchè della fatal quiete
Tu sei l'immago, a me sì cara vieni,
O Sera! E quando ti corteggian liete
Le nubi estive e i zeffiri sereni,

E quando dal nevoso aere inquiete
Tenebre e lunghe all'universo meni,
Sempre scendi invocata, e le secrete
Vie del mio cor soavemente tieni.

Vagar mi fai co' miei pensier su l'orme
Che vanno al nulla eterno; e tanto fugge
Questo reo tempo, e van con lui le torme

Delle cure onde meco egli si strugge;
E mentre io guardo la tua pace, dorme
Quello spirto guerrier ch'entro mi rugge.

UGO FOSCOLO

The Sepulchres

From the days when first the nuptial feast, and judgment seat,
And altar, softened our untutor'd race,
And taught to man his own and others' weal,
The living treasured from the bleaching storm
And savage brute, those sad and poor remains
By nature destined to a lofty fate.
Then tombs became the witnesses of pride,
And altars for the young: thence gods invoked,
Uttered their solemn answers; and the oath
Sworn on the father's dust was thrice revered.
Hence the devotion, which with various rites,
The warmth of patriot virtue, kindred love,
Transmits us through the countless lapse of years.
Not in those times did stones sepulchral pave
The temple floors — . . . But in living green
Cypress and stately cedar spread their shade
O'er unforgotten graves, scattering in air
Their grateful odors; vases rich received
The mourners' votive tears. There pious friends
Enticed the day's pure beam to gild the gloom
Of monuments — for man his dying eye
Turns ever to the sun; and every breast
Heaves its last sigh toward the departing light!
There fountains flung aloft their silvery spray,
Watering sweet amaranths and violets
Upon the funeral sod; and he who came
To commune with the dead, breathed fragrance round,
Like bland airs wafted from Elysian fields.

Translated by E. F. ELLET

Dal dì che nozze tribunali ed are
Dier alle umane belve esser pietose
Di sè stesse e d'altrui, toglieano i vivi
All'etere maligno ed alle fere
I miserandi avanzi, che Natura,
Con veci eterne, a sensi altri destina.
Testimonianza a' fasti eran le tombe,
Ed are a' figli; e uscian quindi i responsi
De' domestici Lari, e fu temuto
Su la polve degli avi il giuramento:
Religion che con diversi riti
Le virtù patrie e la pietà congiunta
Tradussero per lungo ordine d'anni.
Non sempre i sassi sepolcrali a' templi
Fean pavimento; . . . Ma cipressi e cedri,
Di puri effluvi i zefiri impregnando,
Perenne verde protendean su l'urne
Per memoria perenne, e preziosi
Vasi accogliean le lacrime votive.
Rapian gli amici una favilla al Sole
A illuminar la sotterranea notte,
Perchè gli occhi dell'uomo cercan morendo,
Il Sole; e tutti l'ultimo sospiro
Mandano i petti alla fuggente luce.
Le fontane versando acque lustrali
Amaranti educavano e viole
Sulla funebre zolla; e chi sedea
A libar latte e a raccontar sue pene
Ai cari estinti, una fragranza intorno
Sentia qual d'aura de' beati Elisi.

UGO FOSCOLO

The Infinite

This lonely knoll was ever dear to me
And this hedgerow that hides from view
So large a part of the remote horizon.
But as I sit and gaze my thought conceives
Interminable spaces lying beyond
And supernatural silences
And profoundest calm, until my heart
Almost becomes dismayed. And as I hear
The wind come rustling through these leaves,
I find myself comparing to this voice
That infinite silence: and I recall eternity
And all the ages that are dead
And the living presence and its sounds. And so
In this immensity my thought is drowned:
And in this sea is foundering sweet to me.

Translated by Jean-Pierre Barricelli

Giacomo Leopardi (1798-1837) is often considered the greatest Italian poet since Dante. As a child he was uncommonly precocious, and by the age of seventeen, almost exclusively through self-study, mastered Latin, Greek, Hebrew, French, and English. But the labors of excessive study permanently impaired his health and left him deformed. His poetry reflects a grim pessimism as a result of his own suffering and his sensitivity to the tragic condition of much of humanity. We present three selections from his Canti *(Songs). In* L'Infinito *the poet becomes mystically enraptured on contemplating the infiniteness of time and space. The message of* Il sabato del villaggio *(slightly abridged) is that the anticipation of a holiday may yield greater pleasure than the holiday itself. Its final verses tenderly admonish a child to make the most of his blissful age of carefree play lest his anticipated festival (adulthood) prove grievous. As for* A sè stesso, *it is doubtful that anyone has ever sounded a greater depth of despair in verse.*

Sempre caro mi fu quest'ermo colle,
E questa siepe, che da tanta parte
Dell'ultimo orizzonte il guardo esclude.
Ma sedendo e mirando, interminati
Spazi di là da quella, e sovrumani
Silenzi, e profondissima quiete
Io nel pensier mi fingo; ove per poco
Il cor non si spaura. E come il vento
Odo stormir tra queste piante, io quello
Infinito silenzio a questa voce
Vo comparando: e mi sovvien l'eterno,
E le morte stagioni, e la presente
E viva, e il suon di lei. Così tra questa
Immensità s'annega il pensier mio:
E il naufragar m'è dolce in questo mare.

GIACOMO LEOPARDI

The maiden comes home from the fields,
At about sunset time,
With her truss of hay; and in her hand
She holds a bunch of violets and roses,
With which, as is her wont,
For tomorrow's holiday,
She will adorn her bosom and her hair.
The old woman sits
Spinning on the steps among her neighbors,
Facing toward the ebbing light of day;
Recounting tales of her past youth,
When she too adorned herself for holidays, . . .
Now the vesper bell proclaims
The holiday's approach;
And at that sound each heart,
It seems, feels comforted.
Children in shouting groups
About the village square
Are leaping here and there
And make a merry din:
Meanwhile the ploughman, whistling, comes home
To his frugal table,
And thinks about his coming day of rest.

Then when every other light around is quenched,
And other sounds are stilled,
You hear the hammer's blow, you hear the saw
Of the carpenter, awake
In his closed shop by lamplight working,
And he works in haste
To end his task before the dawning glow.

Of all seven, this day is most welcome,
Filled with hope and joy:

La donzelletta vien dalla campagna,
In sul calar del sole,
Col su fascio dell'erba; e reca in mano
Un mazzolin di rose e di viole
Onde, siccome suole,
Ornare ella si appresta
Dimani, al dì di festa, il petto e il crine.
Siede con le vicine
Su la scala a filar la vecchierella,
Incontro là dove si perde il giorno;
E novellando vien del suo buon tempo,
Quando ai dì della festa ella si ornava, . . .
Or la squilla dà segno
Della festa che viene;
Ed a quel suon diresti
Che il cor si riconforta.
I fanciulli gridando
Su la piazzuola in frotta,
E qua e là saltando,
Fanno un lieto romore:
E intanto riede alla su a parca mensa,
Fischiando, il zappatore,
E seco pensa al dì del suo riposo.

Poi quando intorno e spenta ogni altra face,
E tutto l'altro tace,
Odi il martel picchiare, odi la sega
Del legnaiuol, che veglia
Nella chiusa bottega alla lucerna,
E s'affretta, e s'adopra
Di fornir l'opra anzi il chiarir dell'alba.

Questo di sette è il più gradito giorno,
Pien di speme e di gioia:

Tomorrow's hours will bring back
Sadness and ennui, and in his thoughts
Each will revert to his accustomed drudgery.

Frolicsome little boy,
This flowering age of yours
Is like a day replete with gladness,
A day serene, and clear,
Forerunner of life's festival.
Be happy, little boy; this is a time
Of joy, a kindly state.
More I shall not say; but if your festival
Be somewhat late to come, let that not grieve you.

Translated by JEAN-PIERRE BARRICELLI

To Himself

Now thou shalt rest forever,
O weary heart! The last deceit is ended,
For I believed myself immortal. Cherished
Hopes, and beloved delusions,
And longings to be deluded, — all are perished!
Rest thee forever! Oh, greatly,
Heart, hast thou palpitated. There is nothing
Worthy to move thee more, nor is earth worthy
Thy sighs. For life is only
Bitterness and vexation; earth is only
A heap of dust. So rest thee!
Despair for the last time. To our race Fortune
Never gave any gift but death. Disdain, then,
Thyself and Nature and the Power
Occultly reigning to the common ruin:
Scorn, heart, the infinite emptiness of all things.

Translated by W. D. HOWELLS

Diman tristezza e noia
Recheran l'ore, ed al travaglìo usato
Ciascun in suo pensier farà ritorno.

Garzoncello scherzoso,
Cotesta età fiorita
E come un giorno d'allegrezza pieno,
Giorno chiaro, sereno,
Che precorre alla festa di tua vita.
Godi, fanciullo mio; stato soave,
Stagion lieta è cotesta.
Altro dirti non vo'; ma la tua festa
Ch'anco tardi a venir non ti sia grave.

GIACOMO LEOPARDI

A ſè ſteſſo

Or poserai per sempre,
Stanco mio cor. Perì l'inganno estremo,
Ch'eterno io mi credei. Perì. Ben sento,
In noi di cari inganni,
Non che la speme, il desiderio è spento.
Posa per sempre. Assai
Palpitasti. Non val cosa nessuna
I moti tuoi, nè di sospiri è degna
La terra. Amaro e noia
La vita, altro mai nulla; e fango è il mondo.
T'acqueta omai. Dispersa
L'ultima volta. Al gener nostro il fato
Non donò che il morire. Omai disprezza
Te, la natura, il brutto
Poter che, ascoso, a comun danno impera,
E l'infinita vanità del tutto.

GIACOMO LEOPARDI

The Fifth of May (1821)

He is no more. So motionless,
Having breathed his last,
Lay his insensitive corpse
Despoiled of so great a soul,
As was the shocked and perplexed
World on hearing the news; . . .

While he sat in splendor on his throne
My poet's fancy beheld him but kept silent . . .
It is now stirred by the sudden
Extinction of so great a radiance
And releases to his tomb a hymn
That, perhaps, is not destined to die.

From the Alps to the Pyramids,
From the Manzanares to the Rhine,
The thunderbolt of that decisive man
Straightway followed his lightning.
It struck from Scylla to the Don
And from sea to sea.

Was it true glory? To posterity
The difficult judgment falls. As for us,
Let us bow our heads to the Supreme
Creator, who wished on that man
Of His own creative spirit
To impress a deeper mark.

Translated by A. M. D.

Alessandro Manzoni (1785-1873) is universally famous for his monumental novel, I Promessi Sposi (The Betrothed). *He also wrote a large number of poetic compositions. Central to Manzoni's thought is a deep religious faith and a reliance on Divine Providence. Exemplary of this is* Il Cinque Maggio (1821), *inspired by the death of Napoleon at St. Helena. The complete poem contains eighteen stanzas.*

Ei fu. Siccome immobile,
Dato il mortal sospiro,
Stette la spoglia immemore
Orba di tanto spiro,
Così percossa, attonita
La Terra al nunzio sta, . . .

Lui folgorante in solio
Vide il mio genio e tacque: . . .
Sorge or commosso al subito
Sparir di tanto raggio:
E scioglie all'urna un cantico
Che forse non morrà

Dall'Alpi alle Piramidi,
Dal Manzanarre al Reno,
Di quel securo il fulmine
Tenea dietro al baleno,
Scoppiò da Scilla al Tanai,
Dall'uno all'altro mar.

Fu vera gloria? Ai posteri
L'ardua sentenza: nui
Chiniam la fronte al Massimo
Fattor, che volle in lui
Del creator suo spirito
Più vasta orma stampar.

ALESSANDRO MANZONI

The Steam-Powered Guillotine

They've made in China
A steam-powered engine
To drive the guillotine:
In three hours this machine
Can pack a hundred thousand heads
Neatly in a row.

The instrument has caused a furor
And their priests have predicted
That the country little by little
To civilization will be addicted;
Left behind like a bag of beans
Will be the Europeans . . .

There was a rebellious people
That paid with heavy heart
Its property and import taxes:
The emperor benign
In that country has tested
The new method.

The virtues of the instrument
A pension have earned
For that executioner of talent
With his invention patent
And they've made him Mandarin
Of Peking.

A monk shouts: A fine thing! . . .
They're even going to baptize him!

Translated by W. G.

Giuseppe Giusti (1806-1850) is known principally for his humorous poetry, which satirizes the decadent mores and the cruel, selfish princes and politicians of his time. Ten lines have been omitted from this poem.

Hanno fatto nella China
Una macchina a vapore
Per mandar la guigliottina:
Questa macchina in tre ore
Fa la testa a cento mila
Messi in fila.

L'istrumento ha fatto chiasso,
E quei preti han presagito
Che il paese passo passo
Sarà presto incivilito;
Rimarrà come un babbeo
L'Europeo . . .

V' era un popolo ribelle
Che pagava a malincuore
I catasti e le gabelle:
Il benigno imperatore
Ha provato in quel paese
Quest'arnese.

La virtù dell'istrumento
Ha fruttato una pensione
A quel boia di talento,
Col brevetto d'invenzione,
E l'ha fatto Mandarino
Di Pekino.

Grida un frate: oh! bella cosa! . . .
Gli va dato anco il battesimo!

GIUSEPPE GIUSTI

Ancient Lament

The tree toward which you'd stretch
Your little child's hand,
The green pomegranate
With the pretty scarlet flowers,

In the silent, lonely garden
Has just burst into bloom again,
And June is restoring it
With its light and warmth.

You, blossom of my tree,
Smitten and withered,
You of my now useless life
Last and only flower,

Are in the cold earth,
Are in the black earth;
No more will the sun cheer you,
Nor will you be awakened by love.

Translated by A. M. D.

Giosuè Carducci (1835-1907) was the dominant figure of Italian poetry in the last quarter of the nineteenth century. A passionate love of his country and an impatience with its ills in the period following unification inspired much of his early poetry. As his nationalistic ardor settled, his poetry, which was deeply inspired by classical civilization and by a sensitivity to nature, acquired truly superlative qualities. In 1906 he received the Nobel Prize for literature. The beauty of the five short poems reproduced here must be sought in the messages he derived from nature. These may be personal, as in Pianto antico, Traversando la Maremma Toscana, *and* Nevicata; *or of broad external significance, as in* Il bove *and* Mezzogiorno alpino.

L'albero a cui tendevi
La pargoletta mano,
Il verde melograno
Da' bei vermigli fior,

Nel muto orto solingo
Rinverdì tutto or ora,
E giugno lo ristora
Di luce e di calor.

Tu fior de la mia pianta
Percossa e inaridita,
Tu de l'inutil vita
Estremo unico fior,

Sei ne la terra fredda,
Sei ne la terra negra;
Nè il sol più ti rallegra
Nè ti risveglia amor.

Giosuè Carducci

Crossing the Tuscan Maremma

Sweet country, whose wild loveliness sank deep
Into my being, inspired my proud free song,
Gave me a heart, where hate and love ne'er sleep,
One glimpse of thee — again my pulse beats strong.

The hills, that still their wonted outline keep,
I recognise again; the dreams, that long
Ago I dreamed, bid me half smile, half weep;
And youth's enchanted visions about me throng.

Ah, all I dreamed and all I loved was vain!
Run as I might, I never reached the goal:
And I shall fall tomorrow; yet once again

The clouds that o'er thy distant hill-tops roll,
Thy fields that glisten through the morning rain,
Whisper of peace unto my storm-tossed soul.

Translated by G. L. BICKERSTETH

Alpine Afternoon

In the great circle of the Alps, over granite
Bleak and drab, over glaciers brightly glowing,
Rules serene, intense and infinite
In its immense silence the noon of day.

Pines and firs, not a gust of wind blowing,
Stand erect in the penetrating sunlight;
One hears the lyre-like prattle only, ever so slight,
Of water that among stones thinly made its way.

Translated by A. M. D.

Dolce paese, onde portai conforme
L'abito fiero e lo sdegnoso canto
E il petto ov'odio e amor mai non s'addorme,
Pur ti riveggo, e il cuor mi balza in tanto.

Ben riconosco in te le usate forme
Con gli occhi incerti tra 'l sorriso e il pianto,
E in quelle seguo de' miei sogni l'orme
Erranti dietro il giovenile incanto.

Oh, quel che amai, quel che sognai, fu in vano;
E sempre corsi, e mai non giunsi il fine;
E dimani cadrò. Ma di lontano

Pace dicono al cuor le tue colline
Con le nebbie sfumanti e il verde piano
Ridente ne le pioggie mattutine.

Giosuè Carducci

Mezzogiorno alpino

Nel gran cerchio de l'alpi, su 'l granito
Squallido e scialbo, su' ghiacciai candenti,
Regna sereno intenso ed infinito
Nel suo grande silenzio il mezzodì.

Pini ed abeti senza aura di venti
Si drizzano nel sol che gli penetra,
Sola garrisce in picciol suon di cetra
L'acqua che tenue tra i sassi flui.

Giosuè Carducci

The Ox

I love thee, pious ox; a gentle feeling
Of vigour and of peace thou giv'st my heart.
How solemn, like a monument, thou art!
Over wide fertile fields thy calm gaze stealing,

Unto the yoke with grave contentment kneeling,
To man's quick work thou dost thy strength impart.
He shouts and goads, and answering thy smart,
Thou turn'st on him thy patient eyes appealing.

From thy broad nostrils, black and wet, arise
Thy breath's soft fumes; and on the still air swells,
Like happy hymn, thy lowing's mellow strain.

In the grave sweetness of thy tranquil eyes
Of emerald, broad and still reflected dwells
All the divine green silence of the plain.

Translated by Frank Sewall

A Snow-Storm

Large, slow snowflakes fall from an ashen heaven: the noisy
Hum and hubbub of life no more go up from the town.
Hushed is the cry of the vendor of herbs, the rumble of waggons,
Hushed are the voices that sang blithely of youth and of love.
Harsh thro' the throbbing air the chimes from the tower o'er the market
Moan, like the sigh of a world far from the daylight withdrawn.
Tap on the frosted panes, birdlike, forlorn, the beloved
Ghosts of old friends who return, calling on me to depart.
Soon, dear ones, very soon—O strong heart, calm thyself—I too
Shall to the silence descend, lay me to rest in the gloom.

Translated by G. L. Bickersteth

T'amo, o pio bove; e mite un sentimento
Di vigore e di pace al cor m'infondi,
O che solenne come un monumento
Tu guardi i campi liberi e fecondi,

O che al giogo inchinandoti contento
L'agil opra de l'uom grave secondi:
Ei t'esorta e ti punge, e tu co 'l lento
Giro de' pazienti occhi rispondi.

Da la larga narice umida e nera
Fuma il tuo spirto, e come un inno lieto
Il mugghio nel sereno aer si perde;

E del grave occhio glauco entro l'austera
Dolcezza si rispecchia ampio e quieto
Il divino del pian silenzio verde.

GIOSUÈ CARDUCCI

Nevicata

Lenta fiocca la neve pe 'l cielo cinereo: gridi,
Suoni di vita più non salgon da la città,
Non d'erbaiola il grido o corrente rumore di carro,
Non d'amor la canzon ilare e di gioventù.
Da la torre di piazza roche per l'aere l'ore
Gemon, come sospir d'un mondo lungi dal dì.
Picchiano uccelli raminghi a' vetri appannati: gli amici
Spiriti reduci son, guardano e chiamano a me.
In breve, o cari, in breve — tu calmati, indomito cuore
Giù al silenzio verrò, ne l'ombra riposerò.

GIOSUÈ CARDUCCI

The Night Jasmine

The flowers of the night are unfolding
At the hour when I think of my dear ones.
   In and out among the viburnums
   Flit the butterflies of the night.
Long since now, the outcries ceased sounding:
Alone there one house still is whispering.
   Nests are slumbering under the winglets,
   Eyes are slumbering under their lids.
From wide open calyx is breathing
The odor of strawberries crimson.
   Brightly burns a light in the room there.
   Grass is glowing over the ditch.
A bee, the late comer, is buzzing
That finds the cells taken already.
   Slowly across the blue stretch of heaven
   Strays the Pleiad hen with her brood.
Through all the long night time the fragrance
That mounts on the breeze is exhaling.
   Upward mounts the light o'er the stairway,
   Beams forth brightly above, and is gone.
'Tis daybreak. The petals, crushed lightly,
Are folding themselves; there is brooding
   Deep within them, soft and mysterious
   No one knows what rapture undreamed.

Translated by ARLETTA M. ABBOTT

A rare talent for exploiting all the beauties of sound distinguishes the poetry of Giovanni Pascoli (1855-1912). He made extensive use of alliteration and unusual word combinations to capture the most intimate meanings of nature. Our chosen poem is like a nocturne pulsating with a sensuous hidden life.

E s'aprono i fiori notturni,
Nell'ora che penso a' miei cari.
    Sono apparse in mezzo ai viburni
    Le farfalle crepuscolari.
Da un pezzo si tacquero i gridi:
Là sola una casa bisbiglia.
    Sotto l'ali dormono i nidi,
    Come gli occhi sotto le ciglia.
Dai calici aperti si esala
L'odore di fragole rosse.
    Splende un lume la nella sala.
    Nasce l'erba sopra le fosse.
Un'ape tardiva sussura
Trovando già prese le celle.
    La Chioccetta per l'aia azzurra
    Va col suo pigolio di stelle.
Per tutta la notte s'esala
L'odore che passa col vento.
    Passa il lume su per la scala;
    Brilla al primo piano: s'è spento . . .
È l'alba: si chiudono i petali
Un poco gualciti; si cova,
    Dentro l'urna molle e segreta,
    Non so che felicità nuova.

GIOVANNI PASCOLI

Crescent Moon

Oh crescent of the waning moon
That glitters on the solitary waters,
Oh silvery sickle, what harvest of dreams
Undulates here under your soft glimmer!

The quick breathing of leaves,
The deep sighs of forest flowers
Are wafted to the sea: no song, no cry,
No sound the vast silence breaks.

Overcome with love and pleasures
The world of the living sleeps . . .
Oh waning sickle, what harvest of dreams
Undulates here under your soft glimmer!

Translated by W. G.

Gabriele D'Annunzio (1863-1938), poet, novelist, dramatist, soldier—whose poetry reflects his life—unconventional, dramatic, colorful, passionate, and sensual, is a virtuoso of words and images, as in the above complete poem and in the exquisite verses of La pioggia nel pineto *(The Rain in the Pine Grove), the first half of which is presented on the following pages. The repetition of some lines in the second part of the selection enhances the sensation of falling rain so vividly conjured throughout the verse.*

O falce di luna calante
Che brilli su l'acque deserte,
O falce d'argento, qual messe di sogni
Ondeggia al tuo mite chiarore qua giù!

Aneliti brevi di foglie,
Sospiri di fiori dal bosco
Esalano al mare: non canto non grido
Non suono pe 'l vasto silenzio va.

Oppresso d'amor, di piacere,
Il popol de' vivi s'addorme . . .
O falce calante, qual messe di sogni
Ondeggia al tuo mite chiarore qua giù!

GABRIELE D'ANNUNZIO

You keep silent. On the threshold
of the forest I don't hear
the words you say,
human words, but I do hear
new words
which raindrops and leaves utter
far away.
Listen. Rain falls
from the scattered clouds.
It falls on the tamerisks
salt-laden and parched,
it falls on the pines
scaly and straight,
it falls on the myrtle
sacred to Venus,
on the broom plant, refulgent
with clusters of flowers,
on the juniper thick
with fragrant berries,
it falls on our faces
sylvan faces,
it falls on our hands
naked hands,
on our clothing
light clothing,
on the fresh thoughts
our souls unfold
new souls,
on the beautiful tale
that yesterday
beguiled you, that today beguiles me,
Oh Hermione.

You hear? The rain falls
on the lonely
verdure
with a patter that endures
and varies in the air
according to the leaves,
some thick, some thin.
Listen. An answer
to the weeping is the singing
of the cicada
whom the southern lament
does not terrify,
nor the ashen sky.
And the pine
has one sound, and the myrtle
another sound, and the juniper
yet another, instruments
diverse
under innumerable fingers.
And immersed
are we in the spirit
of the wood-land,
pulsating with arboreal life:
and your inebriated face
is moist with rain
like a leaf,
and your tresses
are fragrant like
the bright broom plant,
oh terrestrial creature
by name
Hermione.

Translated by W. G.

Taci. Su le soglie
del bosco non odo
parole che dici
umane; ma odo
parole più nuove
che parlano gocciole e foglie
lontane.
Ascolta. Piove
dalle nuvole sparse.
Piove su le tamerici
salmastre ed arse,
piove su i pini
scagliosi ed irti,
piove su i mirti
divini,
su le ginestre fulgenti
di fiori accolti,
su i ginepri folti
di coccole aulenti,
piove su i nostri volti
silvani,
piove su le nostre mani
ignude,
su i nostri vestimenti
leggieri,
su i freschi pensieri
che l'anima schiude
novella,
su la favola bella
che ieri
t'illuse, che oggi m'illude,
o Ermione.

Odi? La pioggia cade
su la solitaria
verdura
con un crepitio che dura
e varia nell'aria
secondo le fronde
più rade, men rade.
Ascolta. Risponde
al pianto il canto
delle cicale
che il pianto australe
non impaura,
nè il ciel cinerino.
E il pino
ha un suono, e il mirto
altro suono, e il ginepro
altro ancora, stromenti
diversi
sotto innumerevoli dita.
E immersi
noi siam nello spirto
silvestre,
d'arborea vita viventi:
e il tuo volto ebro
e molle di pioggia
come una foglia,
e le tue chiome
auliscono come
le chiare ginestre,
o creatura terrestre
che hai nome
Ermione.

GABRIELE D'ANNUNZIO

On the Threshold

My heart, little lad full of mirth, whose laughter breaks even through tears,
My heart, but an urchin in years, so happy to live on this earth,
Shut close in your niche softly napping, you hear, I am sure, on strange mission,
Someone at your door who keeps tapping and tapping?—It is the physician.
He taps me in rhythmic notation; he holds, I know not on what quest,
To the front and the back of my chest, machinery of auscultation.
Now what does he hear, the old faker? They almost would move me to laughter,
His airs of a skilful wiseacre, were it not for the bill to come after.
"I catch a slight whisper away on the apex—not much, just a clue."
And with his ridiculous crayon he draws a small circle of blue.
"High feeding, no more versifying, no more of your 'white nights' passed waking,
No more cigarettes, no love-making—some climate that's drier, less trying,
San Remo perhaps, or Rapallo—no depression, take things with a laugh.
Then, if you permit, we shall follow our search with the radiograph."

My heart, little lad full of mirth, whose laughter breaks even through tears,
My heart, but an urchin in years, so happy to live on this earth.
O heart, my suspicion is keen (for your sake alone I spend breath
In grieving), there draws nigh that Queen whom mortals denominate Death . . .
A Lady with no shape or form, a Lady in nothingness dressed,
Wherever her cold fingers rest, she touches things but to transform.
You'll feel, heart, well-being throughout, a light load, without pain or care,
You'll waken quite altered without—in name and in face and in hair.
You'll waken in corpore sano, to feel yourself different, unmembered,
The colloquies no more remembered you held with that guidogozzano . . .

Translated by RUTH SHEPARD PHELPS

Guido Gozzano (1883-1916), afflicted with tuberculosis from early childhood, passionately loved life. In the above dialogue with his heart he accepts with smiling indifference, gentle irony, and resignation the knowledge of his early end.

Mio cuore, monello giocondo che ride pur anco nel pianto,
Mio cuore, bambino che è tanto felice d'esistere al mondo,
Pur chiuso nella tua nicchia, ti pare sentire di fuori
Sovente qualcuno che picchia, che picchia . . . Sono i dottori.
Mi picchiano in vario lor metro spiando non so quali segni,
M'auscultano con li ordegni il petto davanti e di dietro.
E senton chi sa quali tarli i vecchi saputi . . . A che scopo?
Sorridere quasi, se dopo non bisognasse pagarli . . .
"Appena un lieve sussurro all'apice . . . qui . . . la clavicola . . ."
E con la matita ridicola disegnano un circolo azzurro.
"Nutrirsi . . . non fare più versi . . . nessuna notte più insonne . . .
Non più sigarette . . . non libri . . . tentare bei cieli più tersi:
Nervi . . . Rapallo . . . San Remo . . . cacciare la malinconia;
E, se permette, faremo qualche radioscopia."

Mio cuore monello giocondo che ride pur anco nel pianto,
Mio cuore, bambino che è tanto felice d'esistere al mondo,
Mio cuore dubito forte — ma per te solo m'accora —
Che venga quella Signora dall'uomo detta la Morte.
È una Signora vestita di nulla e che non ha forma.
Protende su tutto le dita, e tutto che tocca trasforma.
Tu senti un benessere, come un incubo senza dolori;
Ti svegli mutato di fuori, nel volto nel pelo nel nome.
Ti svegli dagl' incubi innocui, diversi ti senti, lontano;
Nè più ti ricordi i colloqui tenuti con guidogozzano . . .

GUIDO GOZZANO

The Ailing Fountain

Clof, clop, clok,
cloffity,
cloppity
clockity.
ckckck . . .

Down in the
courtyard
is the poor
ailing
fountain,
such anguish
to hear it
cough!
It coughs,
and coughs,
for a while
it is silent,
then again
it coughs.
Poor fountain
of mine,
you're ailing
and wringing
my heart.

Silence,
not a drop
from the spout,
silence,
no sound

at all
is heard,
perhaps . . .
it is dead?
Oh, horror!
Ah, no!
There,
again,
it coughs.

Clof, clop, clok,
cloffity,
cloppity,
clockity,
ckckck . . .

Consumption
is killing her.
Heavens,
its eternal
coughing
is death
to me,
a little
is fine,
but so much!
Such whining!
Habel!
Victoria!
Do run,
shut off

the fountain,
its eternal
coughing
is killing
me!
Go, go,
do something,
to make
it stop,
or even . . .
or even
to make it
die!
O Mary!
O Lord!
No more,
no more!
Poor fountain
of mine,
your illness
you'll see,
will be
also
the death
of me.

Clof, clop, clok,
cloffity,
cloppity,
clockity,
ckckck . . .

Translated by CARLO L. GOLINO

Aldo Palazzeschi (1885-) is a first rate novelist who began his career as a poet. An ironical good humor pervades his delightful verse. This is his best known poem.

Clof, clop, cloch,
cloffete,
cloppete,
clocchete,
chchch . . .

È giù
nel cortile
la povera
fontana
malata:
che spasimo
sentirla
tossire!
Tossisce,
tossisce,
un poco
si tace . . .
di nuovo
tossisce.
Mia povera
fontana,
il male
che hai
il cuore
mi preme.

Si tace,
non getta
più nulla,
si tace
non s'ode

rumore
di sorta.
Che forse . . .
sia morta?
Che orrore!
Ah, no!
Rieccola,
ancora tossisce.

Clof, clop, cloch,
cloffete,
cloppete,
clocchete,
chchch . . .

La tisi
l'uccide.
Dio santo,
quel suo
eterno
tossire
mi fa
morire,
un poco
va bene
ma tanto . . .
Che lagno!
Ma Habel!
Vittoria!
Andate,
correte,
chiudete

la fonte:
mi uccide
quel suo
eterno
tossire!
Andate,
mettete
qualcosa
per farla
finire,
magari . . .
Magari
morire.
Madonna!
Gesù!
Non più
non più!
Mia povera
fontana,
col male
che hai,
finisce,
vedrai,
che uccidi
me pure.

Clof, clop, cloch,
cloffete,
cloppete,
clocchete,
chchch . . .

ALDO PALAZZESCHI

My Native Land

O native land,
Lost forever.
Paradise in which I lived
Happily, without sin,
Where once my friends were
The hay snakes,
Better friends than humans later.
On sleepless nights
When my heart is most tormented and cries out
And will not rest in peace,
You appear to me and in you I take refuge.
Not memories do I ask of you,
But repose and oblivion.
And after much wandering
I rejoice in finding myself in you,
Native land, for whom I bear
Everlasting fever in my blood.
Evermore am I persuaded that you alone
Have never betrayed me
And that leaving you great folly was.
How distant you are now, so far away!
If only to reach you and annihilate myself in you
Even death would seem to me dear.

Translated by W. G.

Vincenzo Cardarelli (1887-   ) reacted against the decadent poetry of his day and favored a return to classicism, which he cultivated in his own way. His influence was felt on the poetry between the two World Wars. A pessimistic view of the world and a nostalgia for his native region are characteristics of his verse.

Terra mia nativa,
Perduta per sempre.
Paradiso in cui vissi
Felice, senza peccato,
Ed ebbi amiche un tempo
Le biscie fienaiole
Più che gli uomini poi.
Nelle notti d'insonnia,
Quando il mio cuore è più angosciato e grida
E non si vuol dar pace,
Tu mi riappari ed in te mi rifugio.
Non memorie io ti chiedo,
Ma riposo ed oblio.
E dopo tanto errare
Godo in te ritrovarmi,
Terra mia di cui porto
L'immortal febbre nel sangue.
Sempre più per suaso che tu sola
Non m'abbia mai tradito
E che il lasciarti fu grande follia.
Così lontana sei, così lontana! . .
Pur di raggiungerti e annullarmi in te
Anche la morte mi sarebbe cara.

VINCENZO CARDARELLI

The Goat

I have spoken with a goat.
She was alone in the meadow, tied to a post.
Satiated with grass and her coat
rain-sodden, she was bleating.

The incessant bleat I felt blending
with my own grief and I answered,
in mockery first and then after
(for sorrow timeless unending
has but the one unvarying note)
because of the message that came
borne over the field from the goat.

From a goat with semitic muzzle
I heard the lamenting
of all living things and their trouble.

Translated by Thomas G. Bergin

Beginning of Summer

Pain, where are you? I do not see you here;
everything I view is hostile to you. The sun
is gilding the city, it is glimmering on the sea.
Vehicles of all kinds on the shore front
are carrying something or someone here and there.
All is in joyful motion, as if
it were happy to be alive.

Translated by A. M. D.

Umberto Saba (1883-1957), a poet who was deeply sensitive to human suffering, never became embittered, for he recognized a certain legitimacy in life's afflictions. In the first poem, the goat symbolizes eternally anguished humanity, whose pain is similar to that of all living things. It is solemnly biblical in tone, but Saba was also capable of expressing a joy of living, as the second selection demonstrates.

Ho parlato a una capra.
Era sola sul prato, era legata.
Sazia d'erbe, bagnata
dalla pioggia, belava.

Quell'uguale belato era fraterno
al mio dolore. Ed io risposi, prima
per celia, poi perchè il dolore è eterno
ha una voce e non varia.
Questa voce sentivo
gemere in una capra solitaria.

In una capra dal viso semita
sentivo querelarsi ogni altro male,
ogni altra vita.

UMBERTO SABA

Principio d'estate

Dolore, dove sei? Qui non ti vedo;
ogni apparenza t'è contraria. Il sole
indora la città, brilla nel mare.
D'ogni sorta veicoli alla riva
portano in giro qualcosa o qualcuno.
Tutto si muove lietamente, come
tutto fosse di esistere felice.

UMBERTO SABA

Morning

I am enlightened
By the immenseness of immensity.

Translated by W.G.

I Am a Creature

Like this rock
of San Michele
so cold
so hard
so desiccated
so impervious
so utterly
unspirited

Like this rock
are my tears
you cannot see

Death
we redeem
by living

Translated by Lowry Nelson, Jr.

Giuseppe Ungaretti (1888-   ) was a polemical figure at first, but he is now firmly established as one of Italy's most distinguished avant garde poets. The mystery of life and the anguish of survival are recurring themes in his poetry. His language is unadorned and compact. He rejects rhyme, traditional meters, and, frequently, punctuation.

M'illumino
d'immenso

GIUSEPPE UNGARETTI

Sono una creatura

Come questa pietra
del S. Michele
così fredda
così dura
così prosciugata
così refrattaria
così totalmente
disanimata.

Come questa pietra
è il mio pianto
che non si vede.

La morte
si sconta
vivendo.

GIUSEPPE UNGARETTI

Noɟtalgia

When
night is about to fade away
a little before springtime
and rarely
does someone pass

Over Paris thickly floats
a gloomy color
as of weeping

In a corner
of a bridge
I contemplate
the infinite silence
of a young girl
sylph-like

Together
our maladies
are fused

And as if carried away
we remain

Translated by W. G.

*With characteristic brevity, in superb verse form and with care-
fully selected tone color, Ungaretti captures the gloomy spirit of
the ever-present gray atmosphere of Paris.*

Quando
la notte è a svanire
poco prima di primavera
e di rado
qualcuno passa

Su Parigi s'addensa
un oscuro colore
di pianto

In un canto
di ponte
contemplo
l'illimitato silenzio
di una ragazza tenue

Le nostre
malattie
si fondono

E come portati via
si rimane

GIUSEPPE UNGARETTI

To Spend the Afternoon, Pale and Pensive

To spend the afternoon, pale and pensive,
near a searing garden wall,
to listen, among the brambles and the brush,
to the blackbirds' cracklings, the rustles of snakes.

In the cracks of the ground or on the vetch
to watch the lines of red ants
which break up, then become interwoven
atop minuscule stooks.

To observe through boughs the distant
pulsing of the sea's scales
while tremulous creaks rise
of cicadas from the bald peaks.

And, going off in the dazzling sun,
to feel, with sad wonder,
how all life and its travail
are in this following of a wall
which has, on its top, sharp bottle-fragments.

Translated by WILLIAM WEAVER

Eugenio Montale, born in 1896, is Italy's most intellectual contemporary poet. He views life, in much of his work, as a desperate experience without purpose and hope. The above selection is representative of this theme. As the poet walks alongside a garden wall in the enervating heat of a summer's afternoon, he imagines, disconsolately, that all life is such a walk. Any attempt to scale the wall and seek relief within the garden is hazardous because of the broken glass along the wall's top.

Meriggiare pallido e assorto
presso un rovente muro d'orto
ascoltare tra i pruni e gli sterpi
schiocchi di merli, frusci di serpi.

Nelle crepe del suolo o su la veccia
spiar le file di rosse formiche
ch'ora si rompono ed ora s'intrecciano
a sommo di minuscole biche.

Osservare tra frondi il palpitare
lontano di scaglie di mare
mentre si levano tremuli scricchi
di cicale dai calvi picchi.

E andando nel sole che abbaglia
sentire con triste meraviglia
com'è tutta la vita e il suo travaglio
in questo seguitare una muraglia
che ha in cima cocci aguzzi di bottiglia.

Eugenio Montale

And Suddenly It's Evening

Each of us stands alone upon the heart of the earth
transfixed by a beam of sunlight:
and suddenly it's evening.

A Refuge of Nocturnal Birds

High on a cliff there's a twisted pine;
intently it listens into the abyss
with its trunk curved down like a crossbow.

A refuge of nocturnal birds,
in the deepest hours of night it resounds
with the swift fluttering of wings.

Even my heart has a nest
suspended into the darkness, and a voice;
it, too, lies awake listening at night.

Translations by A. M. D.

The poetry of Salvatore Quasimodo (1901-), winner of the Nobel Prize for literature in 1959, is distinguished by two clearly defined periods. The first, which extends roughly from 1920 to the second World War, is characterized by an economical, strictly essential poetic idiom. Despite this he succeeds in creating profoundly personal and compelling images. The two selections on this page belong to his first period. The three verses of Ed è subito sera synthesize with great poignancy the ephemeral nature of the life of man. In the sensitive second poem the poet's heart intently listens in the darkness for poetic messages.

Ognuno sta solo sul cuor della terra
trafitto da un raggio di sole:
ed è subito sera.

Rifugio d'uccelli notturni

In alto c' è un pino distorto;
sta intento ed ascolta l' abisso
col fusto piegato a balestra.

Rifugio d' uccelli notturni,
nell' ora più alta risuona
d'un battere d'ali veloce.

Ha pure un suo nido il mio cuore
sospeso nel buio, una voce;
sta pure in ascolto, la notte.

SALVATORE QUASIMODO

Homecomings

Piazza Navona, at night, on your benches
I would lie on my back in search of quiet,
and my eyes tracing straight lines and curving spirals
linked together the stars,
the same ones I followed as a child
stretched out on the dry stone bed of the Platani
while I scanned my prayers in the dark.

I would clasp my hands under my head
and remember my homecomings:
odors of fruit drying on wicker mats,
of wall flowers, ginger, and lavender;
when I thought of reading to you, but softly,
(just the two of us, mother, in a dimly lighted corner)
the parable of the prodigal son,
which pursued me always in moments of silence
like a rhythm resounding in me persistently,
even against my wishes.

But the dead are not allowed to return,
and there is no time even for your mother
when you hear the call of the road:
I would then set out again, hidden by the night
like one who fears he will never leave if dawn comes.

And the road gave me my songs
which taste of grain ripening on stalks,
of the white olive grove blossoms
that mingle with blue flowers of flax and with jonquils;
rumbling sounds in the whirling road dust,
monotonous chants of men and creaking carts
their dim lanterns swinging,
scarcely as luminous as fireflies.

Translated by A. M. D.

I ritorni *also falls within Quasimodo's first period. It tells of the irresistible call of the road, with its rich promise of poetic inspiration, despite the nostalgia for his beloved mother and his Sicilian homeland.*

Piazza Navona, a notte, sui sedili
stavo supino in cerca della quiete,
e gli occhi con rette e volute di spirali
univano le stelle,
le stesse che seguivo da bambino
disteso sui ciottoli del Platani
sillabando al buio le preghiere.

Sotto il capo incrociavo le mie mani
e ricordavo i ritorni:
odore di frutta che secca sui graticci,
di violacciocca, di zenzero, di spigo;
quando pensavo di leggerti; ma piano,
(io e te, mamma, in un angolo in penombra)
la parabola del prodigo,
che mi seguiva sempre nei silenzi
come un ritmo che s'apra ad ogni passo
senza volerlo.

Ma ai morti non è dato di tornare,
e non c'è tempo nemmeno per la madre
quando chiama la strada:
e ripartivo, chiuso nella notte
come uno che tema all'alba di restare.

E la strada mi dava le canzoni,
che sanno di grano che gonfia nelle spighe,
del fiore che imbianca gli uliveti
tra l'azzurro del lino e le giunchiglie;
risonanze nei vortici di polvere,
cantilene d'uomini e cigolio di traini
con le lanterne che oscillano sparute
ed hanno appena il chiaro d'una lucciola.

SALVATORE QUASIMODO

Soldiers Cry at Night

Neither the Cross nor His childhood image,
not the hammer of Golgotha, nor His angelic
memory will suffice to obliterate war.
Soldiers cry at night
before dying; they are strong; they fall
at the feet of words learned
serving in the army of life.
Loving ciphers, soldiers,
anonymous outpourings of tears.

Translated by A. M. D.

The war brought great changes to Quasimodo's poetry. It be-came more concrete, more committed to the external reality, the human condition, and the analysis of significant events. The above selection from his second period expresses man's inability to eradi-cate war, and in spite of the memory of the Christ Child and His sacrifice on Golgotha on man's behalf, soldiers continue to die in lonely anonymity.

Nè la Croce nè l' infanzia bastano,
il martello del Golgota, l' angelica
memoria a schiantare la guerra.
I soldati piangono di notte
prima di morire, sono forti, cadono
ai piedi di parole imparate
sotte le armi della vita.
Numeri amanti, soldati,
anonimi scrosci di lacrime.

SALVATORE QUASIMODO

To the New Moon

In the beginning God created the heaven
and the earth; then in His exact
day He set the lights in heaven,
and on the seventh day He rested.

After millions of years, man,
made in His image and likeness,
never resting, with his
secular intelligence,
without fear, in the serene sky
of an October night,
set other luminaries like
those that turned
from the creation of the world. Amen.

Translated by ALLEN MANDELBAUM

In Alla nuova luna, *entirely contemporary in inspiration, the poet takes stock of man's spectacular space accomplishments. We have chosen it as a fitting conclusion to this collection which began with* The Canticle of the Lord's Creations, *composed by San Francesco d'Assisi almost eight centuries earlier. Although Quasimodo speaks of man as "made in His image and likeness," no contrast could be more stark than the infinite humility of St. Francis as he thanks the Lord for "sister moon and stars" and the brashness of modern man as he fearlessly launches his own heavenly bodies.*

In principio Dio creò il cielo
e la terra, poi nel suo giorno
esatto mise i luminari in cielo
e al settimo si riposò.

Dopo miliardi di anni l'uomo
fatto a sua immagine e somiglianza,
senza mai riposare, con la sua
intelligenza laica,
senza timore, nel cielo sereno
d'una notte d'ottobre,
mise altri luminari uguali
a quelli che giravano
dalla creazione del mondo. Amen.

SALVATORE QUASIMODO

Index